HERESIES

OF THE

20TH CENTURY

HERESIES OF THE 20TH CENTURY

PHILOSOPHICAL ESSAYS

BY

M. N. ROY

GYAN

Published by

GYAN

Gyan Publishing House
5, Ansari Road
Daryaganj, New Delhi-110002
Phone: 011-47034999, 9811692060
E-mail: books@gyanbooks.com

Distribution Network
gyanbooks.com
India, USA, Canada, UK, Australia

ISBN: 978-93-6280-704-5 (PB)
First Published, 1940

2nd Impression 2024

Printed at: Gyan Press, Delhi.

HERESIES OF THE 20TH CENTURY
Author: M. N. ROY

HERESIES
OF THE
20TH CENTURY

PHILOSOPHICAL ESSAYS

BY

M. N. ROY

PREFACE

This is a collection of critical essays on a variety of philosophical questions Some of them are of long standing, having been discussed throughout the ages Others are of more recent origin and, therefore, are still controversial The philosophical question arising from the discoveries of modern physics are treated very briefly in the essay which appears as the title of the book The concluding chapter is specially written, and, dealing with the most fundamental question of philosophy, rounds up the discussion of a variety of topics in all these essays

All the chapters are self-contained, each dealing with a particular problem or a complex of inter-related problems Nothing need be said about them by way of introduction The only exception is the first essay It deals with the philosophical consequences of modern science, and therefore, in its present form, is bound to be rather fragmentary As a matter of fact, it is a fragment of a bigger book — "The Philosophical

Consequences of Modern Science" — written over a number of years, and expected to be published before long. I wrote the book in jail. Shortly before my release, I came to know of Sir Mohammad Suleiman's thesis bearing the title "Heresies of the Twentieth Century Physics". Having had been engaged for several years in the investigation of the question, whether the discoveries of modern physics really compel the scrapping of the concepts of substance and causality, I was naturally very interested in what Sir Suleiman had to say. I was concerned neither with the technical scientific aspect of the controversy, nor with the mathematical calculations. My concern was with the logical philosophical deductions. Of course, the deductions could be made only from a correct understanding and proper appreciation of the scientific discoveries and of the abstract mathematical language in which they are stated. But the thing in Sir Suleiman's thesis which struck me was that, while insisting that rational thinking would be impossible without the concepts of substance and causality, he pointed out the "heresies of the twentieth century physics" which, also in his opinion, have discarded those concepts. His "new theory of gravitation" or the critique of the theory of relativity were not the subjects of my discussion for the time being, although I incidentally pointed out that his "New Theory of Gravitation" was not an improvement upon

Einstein, but a reversal to Newton. The merits of his mathematics I did not touch at all I only wanted to point out the contradiction between his professed philosophical views and the Eddingtonian appreciation of the consequences of the modern physical theories. The crass contradiction could be explained only by assuming that Sir Suleiman did not take the trouble of approaching the problems independently, having taken on their face value the authoritative views of leading physicists like Eddington, Jeans, Bohr, Heisenberg and others His lectures in presenting his Thesis bore out the assumption Therefore, I thought it would be helpful if someone drew his attention to the fact that the problems could be approached from different angles I did no more than that in my essay, which sought to prove that the discoveries of the twentieth century physics did not make such fundamental concepts of philosophy as substance and causality untenable

Upon the publication of this essay as a series of articles in a periodical, Sir Suleiman was kind to take notice of them, and sent in his reply It was also published as a series of articles in the same journal. But unfortunately, in his reply, Sir Suleiman altogether missed my point He extensively quoted opinions of leading scientists to disprove my contention that modern physics does not discard the concepts of substance and causality Unless the reply meant a repudiation of Sir Suleiman's own view that without those fundamental concepts no rational thinking is possible, it was all pointless Therefore, I did not think it was necessary for me to meet Sir Suleiman's somewhat irrelevant aspersions against Marxism which, in his opinion, had prejudiced my approach to the problems under discussion If Sir Suleiman has changed his philosophical views since he delivered his lectures, then, his position is quite consistent Otherwise, he cannot logically find fault with my appreciation of the philosophical consequences of modern physics My appreciation is that in the light of modern discoveries, the concepts of substance and causality must be re-stated The concepts remain, only new contents must be put into them That is my heresy The heresy, therefore, amounts to a defence of Materialism which, in my opinion, has been reinforced by the discoveries of modern science, instead of being exploded, to be replaced by a neo-spiritualist mysticism

All the old problems treated in the other essays have been approached from this heretical point of view. The judgement about the result is left to the readers.

Dehradun,
December, 1939.

—*M. N Roy.*

"HERESIES"

OF

THE 20TH CENTURY PHYSICS.

Addressing the National Academy of Sciences on the 13th and 14th Chapters of his treatise on "a new gravitational theory", Sir Shah Suleiman spiritedly defended the reality of matter. That is a bold position to take up in these days when authoritative scientists like Eddington have made fashionable the fiction that modern physics has discarded the concepts of substance and causality Sir Suleiman's defence of matter, however, is seriously weakened by his rejection of the theory of relativity which is the technical-scientific thesis of his paper. While on general principle his defence of matter is sound, his criticism of new physical theories is not only fallacious, but appears also to be surprisingly ill-informed Even the soundness of his philosophical position is impaired methodologically.

He rejects the generally accepted results of modern physical research because they imply "negation of philosophy" He seems to take up the indefensible position that the test of the correctness of scientific theories is their conformity with a priori metaphysical concepts No scientist would agree with that Science has outgrown the tutelage of philosophy having found empirical approach to the so-called metaphysical problems, traditionally considered to be the concern of speculative thought Philosophy speculated about them, but never solved them Finally, science has compelled philosophers - those who are not blinded by the zeal for preserving the traditional monopoly - to admit that, if the nature of the contents of a priori metaphysical concepts, such as space, time, substance and causality, could not be revealed a posteriori by the advance of the empirical knowledge of objective reality, they should be discarded as empty abstractions. In other words, metaphysical concepts must be constantly revised in the light of empirical knowledge. A philosophy that disputes this relationship is antagonistic to the spirit of science. That is a system of dogmatic metaphysics, not to be defended by any scientist. Whenever any philosophical doctrine is rendered palpably untenable by verified results of scientific research, it must go Otherwise philosophy could not claim to be the science of sciences—a logical system of knowledge

Now then, if it were true that modern physical research had exposed the concept of matter to be a metaphysical abstraction, devoid of any empirical, physical, ontological content, well, so much the worse for it. There would be no choice It must go That is the position of scientific philosophy But it is not true. Sir Suleiman confuses certain revolutionary discoveries of quantum physics with a popular philosophical interpretation placed on them The rather curious failure to judge the results of quantum physics on their own merit, places him in the position of defending a lost cause The new hypothesis about the structure of matter he advances, grows out of the knowledge of subatomic mechanism It was suggested more than ten years ago by De Broglie, and has since been verified by numerous experimental tests But I shall come to it in due course of this discussion For the moment the point is that, to be relevant, Sir Suleiman's criticism should be directed against the positivist, neo-Machian, interpretation of the results of microcosmic research, instead of the theories of quantum physics themselves. If he agreed with that interpretation, it is difficult to see how he could defend the reality of matter on scientific ground. It is no argument to exclaim matter is dead, long live matter! Nor will the appeal to pure reason do That would be reversion to metaphysics If there is no scientific evidence for the reality of matter, the concept can be plausibly dismissed as a commonsense prejudice. This has been done, for example, by philosophers like Whitehead On the other hand, denial of the objective reality of matter and causality, as represented by Eddington, Bertrand Russell and others is logically sound It can be convincingly refuted only on the evidence of science, on the strength of empirical knowledge In one word, the defence of matter must be ontological Sir Suleman makes the mistake of making his case a matter of logic, and that is as good as throwing up a sound case

Therefore I thought that it might be useful to point out the contradictions of Sir Suleman's position. If these were removed, his defence of matter would be much stronger I fully agree with the philosophical view defended by him, but propose to show that it is reinforced by the revolutionary results of modern physical research, by the very theory of relativity Sir Suleman rejects, as well as by the wave conception of matter on which vital point he seems to be misled by metaphysical interpretations What is the philosophical consequence of modern scientific theories? Having carefully examined all relevant meterials, one must come to the conclusion that the physical content of the philosophical concept of substance stands out more clearly than ever in the revealing light of modern scientific research. The ultimate constituent of matter is an ontological category, an empirical reality One of the fundamental problems of philosophy, hitherto regarded as of metaphysical nature, is solved through the application of the principle of relativity to the microcosmic mechanism

With these preliminary observations I shall turn to the "heresies" condemned by Sir Suleiman, namely, Einstein's denial of the absoluteness of time and "the Schroedinger-Heisenberg denial of the reality of matter" My contention is that science cannot be charged with the latter heresy The charge cannot be brought home against any leading quantum physicist. Neither Schroedinger nor Heisenberg, not even the mystically inclined Bohr, nor the probabilist Born expressely denies the existence of matter. What they maintain is that deep down in the foundation of the structure of the physical world the classical laws of mechanics do not hold good, that the ultimate constituents of matter have no simple location in space.

The significance of this revolutionary discovery is that ultimately the stuff of the world is not a granular substance, that extension in space is not the final test of physical existence Schroedinger is the founder of wave-mechanics which has established De Broglie's hypothesis as regards the dual structure of matter—the new conception of matter suggested by Sir Suleiman himself The heretic, in this case, is Eddington who is not a quantum physicist and the heresy is philosophical rather than scientific He places a philosophical interpretation on the results of subatomic research which includes denial of the reality of matter.

As regards the other "heresy", Einstein would readily own it, because it is not a heresy at all The denial of the absoluteness of time is no more a scientific or philosophical heresy than was the rejection of geocentrism Einstein is a heretic in the sense Copernicus and Galileo were heretics. The theory of relativity empirically establishes the reality of time, instead of denying it. It has replaced a metaphysical ghost by a physical reality The notion of absolute time, that is, time in which nothing happens, is so bizarre that it "cannot be accepted without a complete surrender of one's intelligence" (to borrow Sir Suleiman's words used for the contrary argument). In these days of the 20th century it is superfluous to urge that the metaphysical concept of absoluteness has no place in science. Physical science deals with measurable quantities. The essence of scientific method is to measure The absolute cannot be measured. Therefore it is an empty abstraction, as far as science is concerned, at any rate. It is no better even philosophically. The knock-out blow to this venerable fiction was dealt by the absolute idealist Hegel himself when he declared that "Absolute Being is Absolute Nothing." Absolute time philosophically, then, is timelessness. Sir Suleiman would invoke the authority of Newton. But authority, however great, cannot serve the purpose of scientific argument Besides, absolute space and time figure in the Newtonian system only as hypotheses. Newton assumed the existence of those categories because, under the influence of scholastic tradition, he could not conceive of changing phenomena being existentially ultimate, self-sufficient He identified reality with absoluteness, and regarded measurable distances and durations as appearances of absolute space and time But having postulated the absolute, to square his philosophical conscience, so to say as a scientist, he set it quietly aside, practically forgot all about it, and occupied himself exclusively with geometrical space and physical time. Indeed, as a scientist, Newton was a relativist Moreover, Newtonian absolutism has all along been vigorously combatted by great mathematicians and physicists since Leibritz As a matter of fact, the theory of relativity celebrates the burial of the phantom of absolute space already layed by Mach The disappearance of absolute time logically follows The twin phantoms must stand or fall together

The mathematical portion of critique of the theory of relativity seems to be rather technical - a matter of detail It amounts to that Einstein's calculation of the influence of the sun's gravitational field on rays of light passing through it, is not accurate Einstein certainly would not maintain that the last word has been said in that connection The 1 7" deflection, theoretically predicted by Einstein, was verified by observational data gathered by eclipse expeditions of 1919 and 1922. But subsequent tests showed a discrepancy of about 50 per cent which, however, was ascribed to technical difficulties That was not considered to be a refutation of the theory. On the contrary, the general trend of scientific opinion was that the theory had been definitely established by the results of the expeditions of 1919 and 1922 The decisive factor is the physical phenomenon of the deflection of light, accuracy of the numerical value of the phenomenon is a matter of detail. It can be affected by a variety of extraneous circumstances, which can be only gradually overcome through the development of the technique of observation. The results of the observation of the eclipses of this year and the next year will clarify the situation

The next question is, can the phenomenon be otherwise explained? An affirmative answer would be a serious challenge to Einstein's theory. Sir Suleiman's paper does not seem to contain that challenge His "near" theory appears to be a return to the old Newtonian position. But the deflection of light cannot be explained by the Newtonian theory. As regards the red-shift, the opponents of the theory of relativity have not been able to offer an alternative explanation which can stand even as a plausible hypothesis Although the red displacement is regarded generally as the most direct confirmation of Einstein's theory of gravitation, on this point also there have been discrepancies in the calculations of numerical value. Here the technical difficulties are even greater, because the calculation can be only statistical; hence the inaccuracy of the result Nevertheless, the investigations of Freundlich and others leave little room for legitimate doubt. Then, there is the remarkable confirmation found in the spectrum of the companion of Sirius. It was Eddington who showed that the pronounced red-shift was due to the terrific gravitational pull resulting from the immense density of the star The alternative explanation, Doppler Effect, fits in with Eddington's theory of the expanding universe, so he would not abandon it, unless the evidence in support of the other explanation were overwhelming.

Sir Suleiman's calculation is theoretical Therefore the discrepancies between the numerical values predicted by him and Einstein respectively is a more serious matter Of course, as he himself says, his calculations would merit serious consideration only on their having stood some crucial test But meanwhile, the question is what is the basis of his calculations ? The classical laws of mechanics do not offer the necessary basis To calculate the numerical value of a phenomenon theoretically, it is necessary to have some hypothesis about its cause

Classical theories do not tell why light from distant stars passing by the Sun should bend As regards the red-shift of spectral lines, the position is slightly better Doppler-Effect offers a hypothesis—of dubious nature Before it was discovered that light has mass, the deflection of light rays could not be ascribed to the gravitational pull of the sun, and this discovery belongs to relativity physics. Upon the verification of Einstein's prediction, the opponent of the theory of relativity argued that, on the assumption that light possessed mass, and therefore, inertia, similar prediction could be made on the basis of the Newtonian law of gravitation. As a matter of fact there is a hypothetical formula worked out already in the beginning of the last century by Soldner But according to that formula, the numerical value of the deflection should be about half of that predicted by Einstein So in that case, the discrepancy between the theoretical results obtained from observation, is much larger than in the case of Einstein's prediction. Sir Suleiman's calculation has the merit of approximating some observational results which are about 50% larger than Einstein value But there remains the crucial question what is the basis of his calculation? If he starts from the assumption that light has mass--and there is no other basis for a theoretical calculation--, then, it is difficult to see how he can reject the whole theory of relativity as he most emphatically does His theoretical structure stands on the foundation laid by Einstein's discovery that light has mass The "new theory of gravitation " thus may amount to a more accurate mathematical deduction from the premiss supplied by the physical principle of relativity which itself is empirically derived Einstein's calculations may suffer from slight error which shall have to be rectified, if and when revealed by recurring discrepancies with observational result. Sir Suleiman may have discovered the possible error theoretically. In that sense, the mathematical portions of his paper may be valuable Then, he would be contributing to the theory of relativity, instead of refuting it

But, philosohically, Sir Suleiman rejects the theory of relativity, that is to say, he rejects it as a whole. The philosopher and the mathematician seem to be pulling in opposite directions The technical mathematical aspect of his paper may turn out to be some contribution to the subject That is still to be proved But Sir Suleiman's philosophical position is clear enough, and it is palpably fallacious I shall deal only with that aspect of his paper The theory of relativity is not to be judged by its ability to explain the phenomenon of gravitation or any other single physical process. It is not a physical theory in the technical sense. It is a system of natural philosophy It must be judged as such If a particular critique of the theory is philosophically false, then, the merits of the mathematical apparatus employed for the purpose cannot take us very far in the right direction

The essence of Einstein's theory of gravitation is the elimination of the metaphysical concept of force which figures in the Newtonian system as an elementary indefinable. Newton regarded gravitation as a mechanical phenomenon - an interaction between material bodies and force Immateriality of the latter is implicit in his dualism. The concept of force vitiated Newton's mechanistic natural philosophy, and contributed largely to the philosophical confusion of many a great physicist of the nineteenth century. In the light of conclusive empirical data amassed, through observations and experiments carried on by a great many physicists over quarter of a century, in order to overcome a whole series of theoretical difficulties which appear to defy the Newtonian laws, Einstein found gravitation to be a kinematic phenomenon, an effect produced by moving bodies. The classical concept of matter-in-motion is dualistic. It compels the postulation of an extraneous, that is to say, immaterial agency to cause acceleration Metaphysics casts its confusing shadow on physical knowledge. The kinematic interpretation of gravitational effect frees physics from the dualist concept of matter-in-motion. Movement being a property of matter, the postulation of an extraneous agency becomes superfluous That is the philosophical significance of Einstein's theory of gravitation. The significance is to establish the sovereignty of matter. This could be done only upon the discovery of the relativity of motion; and that discovery logically led to the revision of the concepts of space and time Sir Suleiman's rejection of the theory of relativity therefore is not consistent with his defence of the reality of matter. Since his philosophy is correct, on principle, though reared on fallacious argument, there must be something wrong with his mathematics. On that score, no more need be said here To-day, neither theoretical physics nor pure methematics can be separated from philosophy Therefore philosophical consistency must be the standard

Fundamentally, there does not seem to be anything new in Sir Suleiman's theory. He rejects the idea of four-dimensional continuum as "misinterpretation of the spherical propagation of gravitational influence " So, he regards the gravitational field as a field of force That is reversal to Newtonian position But it is long since that physics has outgrown the pure empiricism of its founders What is gravitational influence? How does it propagate? Why is there such an interaction between bodies, and why is it governed by a mathematical law? How is action at a distance possible?

In course of development, physics was confronted with these formidable questions which could not be satisfactorily answered by the classical theories. Careful study of the " Principia " shows that Newton himself felt that his theory was rather a description than explanation of observed phenomena; that it did not expose their physical cause. This is made clear by the passage in which the famous expression—"hypothesen non-fingo"—occurs The law of inverse square does not tell us anything about the nature of gravitation Force was simply a name for an unknown category. The law was purely empirical. But Newton's genius could not help wondering at the recurring appearance of 'r' in the formula Why always the square and not any other function of 'r'? Mathematical laws are symbolic expressions of invariant physical relations Newton's theory of gravitation did not reveal the physical relation between gravitating bodies That had still to be done The concept of force was like the algebraic symbol *x* It stood for an unknown quantity which had to be discovered Einstein's theory represents that discovery It is the completion of an investigation begun by Newton. Sir Suleiman's " new " gravitational theory, in as much as it is Newtonian, rejects a view of cosmic mechanism which is its own logical culmination!

Though it is hardly necessary, I shall mention the important links in the chain of thought which connects the new theory that gravitational field is a metric field with the classical concept of the field of force

Action at a distance is a physical impossibility. On the other hand, classical mechanics was founded on the concepts of mass-points moving in empty space The difficulty was surmounted by assuming that energy propagated through empty space The assumption was founded on the emission theory of light. The vindication of the undulatory theory by Young and Frensel naturally demanded the postulation of a medium of propagation. Huygens had felt the necessity but hesitated to endow space with the properties of an elastic solid Frensel ventured to assume a pervasive medium with the necessary properties. His attitude was pragmatic The problem was left to be solved eventually Ether occupied a place in physics-to contradict the notion of empty space But its admission, on the other hand, raised a new question what really is the substance the periodic changes of which, or in which, is light ?

While the question remained unanswered the idea of ether was reinforced by the development of the science of electricity. Faraday found that electric and magnetic actions between two bodies were dependent on an intervening medium. He concluded that a field of force (gravitational, electric or magnetic) was not a field of action at a distance; that the interaction of bodies took place through an intermediary.

Though Coulomb's law had pointed to the similarity of electric action and gravitation, Newton's authority precluded the application of Faraday's revolutionary discovery to mechanics generally The final blow to action at a distance was dealt by Maxwell's generalisation of the results of Faraday's experiments. Since effects that take place through a medium are transmitted through space, this must be an electro-magnetic medium The outstanding question about the nature of ether was answered According to Maxwell, any change in an electric or magnetic field propagates in all directions with uniform finite velocity. Thus propagation of energy came to be regarded as propagation of real physical states

Laplace, Gaus and Boisson had mathematically pictured the universe as a net-work of "lines of force." These appeared now as mathematical expressions of electro-magnetic states propagating through space. At the same time, the finiteness of the velocity of light also resulted from Maxwell's equations That again indicated that space could not be really empty. The existence of a pervasive medium theoretically established, it should be possible to ascertain absolute velocity through space. But experiments (of Michelson, Morley and others) gave negative results which could not be explained without ad hoc accessary hypotheses

("Fitzerald-Contraction" and "Lorentz-Transformation") Finally, Einstein suggested that the explanation was to be found in a new theory of Kinematics.

The impossibility of determining absolute velocity showed that "pure motion," mathematically treated in classical dynamics, was a fiction The Special Theory of Relativity laid the foundation for an empirical theory of Kinematics which exposed the underlying connection between gravitation and electro-magnetism. On the one hand, there is no action at a distance and, on the other, space is not filled with a pervasive medium Observed phenomena, described as Fitzerald-Contraction or Lorentz-Transformation, are not produced by a direct physical cause, namely, pressure of a stationary medium (ether), but are Kinematic effects of relative motion That is the physical principle of relativity in the light of which (elaborated in the General Theory) field of force, gravitational as well as electro-magnetic, was later on discovered to be metric-field The "lines of force" of classical physics are Minkowski's "world-lines" which, described by moving bodies, constitute the texture of space. Euclidean geometry won't do for the new conception of space Bolyai, Lobatchewsky and Riemann had already shown the theoretical possibility of non-Euclidian space In the light of Einstein's Kinematics,

"Metageometry", hitherto regarded as a purely speculative construction, appeared as the picture of physical reality. Kinematics became identified with geometry which was merged into physics. Gravitational effects are produced by the structure of space. Gravitational field is a metric-field the potentials of which are determined by the distribution of matter All physical processes are to be traced down to the common foundation of moving bodies Gravitation is a physical phenomenon, an empirical reality, but there is no such thing as gravitational force* acting upon bodies at a distance any more than there is a pervasive medium (ether) for the propagation of energy, unless this is identified with space which itself is physically real only as a function (extendedness) of matter Einstein himself favoured retention of the concept of ether with this content

A really new theory of gravitation must show that it is neither a mechanical phenomenon caused by the operation of an extraneous force, nor a Kinematic effect produced by the relativity of motion The classical view has been discarded in course of the development of physics , and the new, incorporated in the General Theory of Relativity, is the logical out-

---

**Eddington has characterised gravitational force as a "put up job"*

come of the whole process of development. The merging of space and time in four dimensional continuum is not an "artificial method". It is compelled by the necessity of explaining observed facts which cannot be fitted into the classical concepts. Sir Suleiman does not suggest a new hypothesis that offers an alternative (third) explanation. The rejection of the theory of relativity would bring physics back to the problem of reconciling gravitation with electro-magnetism. The return to the idea of the pervasive medium would confront it with the negative result of the experiment for ascertaining absolute velocity.*

Sir Suleiman's theory does not offer any new solution of these theoretical and experimental problems of modern physics Therefore, his rejection of the theory of relativity seems to be rather arbitrary, his critique is evidently artificial. For example, he even falls into the popular mistake of thinking (he says so,

---

** In this connection it may be mentioned that sometime ago Miller repeated the Michelson-Morley experiment on a high mountain, and claimed to have obtained positive results. The claim has been refuted by Picard's experiment in a balloon and those of Thomaschek on the high Alpine peak, Jungfrau. Besides, quantitatively, the results of Miller's experiment does not quite meet the requirements of of the absolutist theory.*

at any rate) that the theory of relativity regards time as the fourth dimension of space which, of course, is not true. Then, in another place, he asserts that Einstein's theory requires property of infinity for the finite velocity of light. It is in the finiteness of the velocity of light, conclusively proved by Maxwell's discovery of its electro-magnetic nature, that Einstein found the decisive evidence against the notion that events throughout the world take place according to one single system of time. The necessity for a new theory of Kinematics (a revision of classical dynamics) results from the demonstration of the facts that finiteness of the velocity of light precludes the determination of absolute motion even through the means of optical or electric processes The finiteness of the velocity of light is the empirical foundation of the physical principle of relativity The negative result of experiments for ascertaining absolute motion shows that c is not a physical constant as Maxwell believed it to be. Einstein argued that it must be regarded as a Kinematic constant, that is to say, the finiteness of the velocity of light is determined by the properties of "empty" space. On the other hand, the fact remains that c is the fundamental constant of electro-magnetism. So, "empty" space need not be filled with an imaginary medium of transmission, being itself an electro-magnetic field the potentiality of which can be measured mathematically, in terms of tensor-impulse. Gravitation is an electro-magnetic phenomenon, and electro-magnetic field is a metric-field Now, it can be seen that even Coulomb's law leads to this, unitary foundation of all physical process. But, it stands out clearly, amenable to mathematical treatment, only when it is reduced to the four-dimensional continuum the intrinsic property of which is expressed by the Kinematic constant c

The critical question is what is the nature of the cause that produces the effect called gravitation ? Newton left the question unanswered. Einstein has given an answer which is empirically well-founded, logically sound, pragmatically successful Therefore, apart from the very weighty consideration that it is an integral part of a whole cosmological conception, Einstein's theory of gravitation stands, unless the opposing theory can give an equally clear and comprehensive answer to the question

Sir Suleiman's theory lacks the merit. It is rather a critique of Einstein's theory than an alternative solution of the problems solved by the theory criticised. As regards the crucial question, Sir Suleiman falls back on the metaphysical concept of force, explicitly as well as implicitly To say that the idea of four-dimensional continuum is a misinterpretation of the spherical propagation of gravitational influence is to hold on to the classical theory of the field of force. If the origin of the field cannot be traced to a physical cause, as is done by exposing it to be a metric-field, "force" must be conceived as a metaphysical category, and that would ruin the case of those who want to defend the reality of matter If physical processes are traced to the exertion of a metaphysical agency, matter can be logically conceived as a mere appearance of the immaterial reality. That was the position of nineteenth century idealism which denied the reality of the world of phenomena Under the influence of that tradition, contemporary scientists like Eddington, Jeans, etc maintain that discovery of the relative nature of its categories space, time, substance and casuality compels to deny the reality of matter. Sir Suleiman's "new" theory of gravitation, thus, is inconsistent with his philosophy. His philosophical criticism of the theory of relativity is equally fallacious. I shall turn to that now.

Sir Suleiman correctly says that time is perceived in two ways, namely, the change of the position of the body, and the change in its state.' He concedes that in the former case, time can, as a mathematical device, be welded together with space in a four-dimensional continuum. But in the latter case, he argues, time demonstrates its absoluteness and complete independence of space His error is the failure to realise that, in the last analysis, the second way is identical with the first, it consists of the sum-total of the changes in the position of the molicules, atoms, and electrons constituting the body, and these are bodies themselves What is the state of a body? A state of physical organisation. According to the classical theory, the physical reality of entities entering into the organisation, consists of their extension in space. Any change in the organisation implies change of the position in space of its constituents So, it is not correct to say that in the second case time is independent of space As a matter of fact, if time ever exists independent of space, it cannot be experienced Therefore, the concept of absolute time leads logically to the denial of the reality of empirical time Classical idealist philosophy draws this logical conclusion. But Sir Suleiman would sit on two stools He would retain the absolutist concept, and prove the existence of time empirically Hence the contradictions of his philosophy If our experience of time is dependent on the changes in the external and internal relations of a body, then the interdependence of time and space is an empirical fact. They are not welded together as a mathematical device, but by nature. To regard them as independent categories, in the sense that either of them can exist by itself, is a metaphysical abstraction. The mathematical device of the theory of relativity purports to express the quantitative value of the objective content of our experience Since space and time are always found mixed up together, to regard them as independent categories is obviously an arbitrary procedure. The question then is, how do these quantitatively distinct categories get so inextricably interwoven ? Relativity physics answers the question, thus helping the solution of a problem that puzzled philosophy for ages. Space and time are not categorical entities, not ultimate realities Not only are they mutually interdependent , they derive their very existence from a common source which ontologically is antecedent to them both They are functions of physical existence. Hence, though quantitatively so different, they are always inextricably mixed up except in abstraction. Even their qualitative distinction is apparent. Fundamentally, they represent the self-same physical reality - extension or extendedness of matter, geometrical and chronological respectively

We find it difficult to grasp this new idea simply because our minds are habituated to flow in an old rut. A little reflection is necessary to realise the remarkable simplicity and logical soundness of the new conception of space and time. Indeed, it is surprising that throughout ages philosophers should have managed to mystify something so obvious Space was postulated as the receptacle of things, because these must be somewhere The primitive logic of naive commonsense made location antecedent to existence Speculative philosophy could never outgrow the primitive logic of its infancy But the fallacy is obvious If things must exist somewhere, space itself must have a location Otherwise, it cannot exist Thus the idea that existence is dependent on location leads to regress ad infinitum. According to the very traditional definition of existence, space does not exist except as extension, and extension logically presupposes something extended This idea about the structure of space is implicit in Euclidean geometry A line is not the integration of the bits of space separating points themselves, and plane is the sum-total of a number of lines Since space is constructed of points, it is a product of existence The function of the point is to exist Existence therefore is antecedent to space

The analysis is equally applicable to the concept of time. Duration also is conditional upon existence. The logic is self-evident A thing must be, in order to become The idea of time is born of the primitive experience of interval between events which are changes in existence Becoming is a string of events constituting the life-history of a thing. Space is being and time is becoming More correctly, space is the measure of being and time that of becoming. While pure being is conceivable, becoming always involves being Thus time can never exist independent of space Nature has welded it together with space.

This simple analysis of the commonsense idea of space and time leads directly to the picture of a four dimensional continuum Being is three-dimensional. But the world is a process of becoming Pure being, that is, eventless existence is an abstraction. Becoming is four-dimensional, because it embraces existence and change, space and time A process of becoming is a four-dimensional continuum. The world picture presented by the theory of relativity is a matter of commonsense and elementary logic. It is not an artificial mathematical construction. Artificial and illogical are the traditional concepts of space and time March of knowledge was bound to reject them

The denial of the absoluteness of time is a heresy from the viewpoint of metaphysical idealism which Sir Suleiman rejects, implicitly at any rate ; otherwise there would be no sense in his defence of the reality of matter. The opposing scientific philosophy of physical realism (or, if I may use the dreadful term, materialism) is reinforced by the achievement of the theory of relativity. Demonstration of the fictitious nature of absolute time establishes the reality of physical time, consequently the final blow is dealt to the venerable philosophical doctrine which regards the phenomenal world as a mere appearance of some mystic, transcendental, metaphysical reality. By declaring the denial of the fiction of absolute time to be a heresy, Sir Suleiman places himself in a philosophical camp where he will be dragged before the holy inquisition for his own heresy - the belief in the reality of matter Evidently, his philosophical position is hopelessly contradictory

As regards physics itself the scrapping of the notion of absolute time is a mere formality For it, time like any other category, must be a measurable entity. Absolute time cannot be measured, therefore with the physicists, it was a metaphysical prejudice Prejudice dies hard, even with the scientists Nevertheless in the face of verified facts, there is no choice, as far as they are concerned. Heresy, that is, to upset traditional beliefs, is the essence of science. All great scientists are heretics. Once it was found that there was no such thing as absolute velocity, the supposition that events in different parts of the universe could be all arranged in one temporal sequence, had to be abandoned Comparison through light signal would not indicate the true interval between events taking place on bodies moving in relation to each other. The rejection of the notion of a universal time is dictated by the discovery that electro-dynamic processes are also subject to the principle of relativity which had been formulated by Newton as regards mechanical motion Einstein showed that the negative result of the Michelson experiment could be explained only by applying the principle of relativity to electro-dynamics He accomplished mathematically a task set before physics by the logic of its own development Therefore, for physics, absolute time is as dead as Queen Anne Only an alternative explanation of the impossibility of determining absolute motion would ever revive it Sir Suleiman does not suggest any such remedy.

The four-dimensional Continuum of the General Theory is the logical outcome of the rejection of the traditional view of time The intervening step was the corresponding revolution in the concept of space which is also a "heresy", from the point of view of metaphysical idealism, because the disappearance of absolute space as well as of absolute time leaves matter as the ultimate constituent of the physical universe. Since in relativity physics, space itself ceases to be a categorical magnitude, it is obviously incorrect to say that time is regarded as a dimension of space This erroneous notion is created by popular expositions of the theory of relativity Minkowski's mathematical restatement of the Kinematics of the Special Theory showed that time could be treated as the fourth member of a system of co-ordinates. That was the mathematical expression of the physical implication of Einstein's Kinematics which subsequently developed into the General Theory. The implication was the inter-dependence of space and time which resulted from the common dependence on matter Minkowski's purely mathematical extension of the Special Theory shows the interdependence of space and time, but does not go to the extent of revealing the cause of that relation. Hence a superficial student may get the impression of time being merged into space; and there results the perplexing idea of four-dimensional space But already in Minkowski's theory space ceases to be stationary The "four dimensional space" is the graphical picture of three dimensional motion The time-function involved in motion appears as the fourth co-ordinate The substance of Minkowski's theory was that the New Kinematics showed the physical possibility of a four dimensional geometry. If a four-dimensional geometry was theoretically possible, space could not be Euclidean, not everywhere, at any rate. But non-Euclidean space is no space; it must be something more than space; therefore, it is four-dimensional The magnitude treated by four-dimensional geometry is not space in the traditional sense , it is a physical continuum - a field of three-dimensional motion Thus motion absorbs not only time, but space also But there is no pure motion. The empirical reality is moving bodies Physically, motion is their mutual relation. In other words, motion is a function of matter Consequently, the "space-like" and "time-like" dimensions are also functions of matter.

The four-dimensional Continuum is a Kinematic totality- an infinite number of the non-Galilian system described by the Special Theory But they are not homogeneous The Kinematics of a particular region is determined by the local distribution of matter It is the fundamental function of matter to create metric fields just as it is the function of a charge of electricity to produce an electric-field, or a magnetic-pole to create a magnetic-field The metric-fields, as Kinematic phenomena, enter into the structure of the four-dimensional Continuum. The hypothesis of the spherical propagation of gravitational influence presupposes homoalloidal space, but the four-dimensional Continuum of the theory of relativity is not a homogeneous structure Therefore, Sir Suleiman's contention that it is a misinterpretation of spherical propagation is groundless Its structure precludes the very idea of uniform propagation c is a Kinematic, not a mechanical, constant It expresses the peculiarity of the structure of "empty space," the peculiarity being that it is not empty Besides, light is not a force, therefore the law of its propagation does not suggest any identity underlying the four-dimensional Continuum and spherical propagation of gravitational force Non-Galilian systems in which gravitational effects appear, are local peculiarities of the Continuum. Gravitation, therefore is not the fundamental law of nature. It is a special case of the law of least interval which is restatement of the fundamental law of the classical mechanics - the law of least interval The four-dimensional Continuum is three-dimensional space filled with action. The physical reality of the four-dimensional Continuum can be deduced from the fact, known to classical dynamics, that action is a product of energy and time.

The full significance of the fact had to be revealed by the theory of relativity. It is the interlocking of space and time as functions of matter. Time cannot be abstracted from energy, nor energy from time, because oscillation is a periodic as well as physical phenomenon. Energy is equivalent to mass; mass implies extension which is the physical equivalent of space On the other hand, Einstein's conversion formula shows that action is not an imaginary magnitude of pure mathematics, but a material entity. The constant of the quantum theory (Planck's Constant) is an atom of action Therefore all energy processes, in the last analysis, are Kinematic effects produced by moving bodies Planck himself, together with many other physicists, did not realise the full significance of his discovery It was believed that quantisation of energy was a boundary condition, and that in the field continuity prevailed The breakdown of the Bohr-model, however, was a blow to the hypothesis that the quantisation of the passage of energy from matter to the field, and vice versa, was determined by inner structure of atom Einstein's theory of light-quantum offered a new solution of the problem energy itself is broken up into quanta - the field is a granular structure Energy is a form of matter.

The minutest fraction of energy, Planck's constant has mass. "Empty space" is filled with energy-impulse. That is the "gravitational force." The infinite number of non-Galilian Kinematic systems, metric fields produced by bodies moving in helical paths under the law of least interval - which enter into the structure of the four-dimensional Continuum, are bound together by "gravitational forces" Only these are not forces at all, but energy-impulse which is a physical magnitude, essentially same as the momentum of the classical theory

In " empty space " the gravitational constant is equal to energy-impulse which is equivalent with the mass of a light quantum. Thus, gravitation ultimately is a function of mass, that is to say, a property of matter, expressed mathematically as energy-impulse which fills space The disappearance of the Riemann Christoffel tensar means no matter, no gravitation, force is nothing but the impulse of motion inherent in matter. The fundamental function of matter is to move. Gravitation is a Kinematic effect produced by relative motion

Those who would still interpret gravitation in terms of force or influence, conceiving this as something extraneous to matter might be reminded of a fact not generally noted The idea of impulse, as it appears in the theory of relativity, was inherent in the fundamental equation of mechanics as originally formulated by Newton. According to Newton, " the impulse of force is equal to the increase in the momentum of the body moved." There is a great difference between this and the text-book formula

"Force is equal to mass times acceleration". However, the point I wish to indicate is that the magnitude entering into the calculations of classical mechanics, is also the impulse of force, not force which is a metaphysical abstraction The magnitude is a physical phenomenon which was explained by the animistic concept of force because it could not be otherwise understood at that time, and the hypothesis worked

The theory of relativity reduces the entire cosmic scheme, including space, time, mass, motion, force, energy, to one single category - matter The ultimate unit of this fundamental reality is conceived as "event", instead of mass-point, in order to lay emphasis on its dynamic character The world is not a static being, it is a process of becoming Therefore, it should be interpreted in terms of "events", that is, of changes in the state of its ultimate constituents Only that way can we get a realistic picture of the cosmic scheme Because "events" are dynamic physical magnitudes, intervals between them are spatial as well as temporal The law of least interval promises to be the quintessence of all the fundamental laws of physics; and the way to the discovery of this law lay through the revolution in the idea of space and time. The defence of the absoluteness of time therefore implies the rejection of the entire theory of relativity. Apart from the fact that the development of physics provided little ground to its scientific opponents, philosophically, the rejection would be throwing away the most conclusive evidence for the reality of matter. So, whatever may be the merit of his "new gravitational theory", philosophically Sir Suleiman takes up the position of hacking down the branch on which he is sitting.

So long as physics and philosophy believed in absolute space and time, regarded these as ultimate categories logically antecedent to being and becoming, the criterion for the reality of matter was simple location Matter was conceived as minute particles of mass occupying discrete positions in space at given moments of time Atomic physics has discovered that matter does not possess these properties, always, in the absolute sense Position and velocity cannot be simultaneously ascertained (Heisenberg's Principle of Uncertainty) The notion of simple location in space must be abandoned If we hold on to the idea that existence is extension in space, then, we must accept the Eddingtonian "heretical" interpretation of the theories of atomic physics Matter does not exist physically because its ultimate units are not extended in space, in the classical absolutist sense.

The solution of the problem is offered by the theory of relativity—it is to be found in the reversal of the relation of matter with space and time Since there is no absolute space, location in space is meaningless So also is the temporal criterion The difficulty results from the application of non-existing standards. In the statement of his Principle of Uncertainty Heisenberg himself makes the position quite clear He says that the difficulty disappears if the classical concepts of space and time are abandoned, (vide, H Heisenberg, "The Physical Principle of the Quantum Theory") The calculation then has to be statistical ; but that is another problem - of determinism - and that also can be solved in the light of the principle of relativity

As regards the New Quantum Theory, it does not imply denial of the reality of matter as such The problem raised by it is about the structure of ultimate substance Philosophically it completes a task begun by the theory of relativity It abolishes the notion of absoluteness regarding the remaining two categories-substance and causality The concept of substance is affected by the revolution in so far as it was identified with mass. Mass is a property of matter (substance); but it is variable like all other properties. The absoluteness of mass disappears already in the theory of relativity. The origin of the wave conception (electric theory) of matter can be traced to Einstein's conversion formula Energy is a form of matter, and this is a vibratory substance Atomic physics has reduced matter to energy That does not mean denial of matter No Quantum physicist denies the existence of atom or of its constituents-electrons and protons The revelation is that these even are not the ultimate units of matter But no serious scientist maintains that measurable entities can emerge out of nothing. The dual structure of matter is not an ad hoc hypothesis It is a mathematically precise theoretical deduction, and has been empirically verified by the experiments of Davison, Germer, Laue, Kikuchi, and others.

If Sir Suleiman's "new conception of matter" (which is not new) differs essentially from the De Broglie hypothesis, which, verified experimentally, showed the way out of the impasse created by the breakdown of Bohr's model, then, it does not reveal the connection between gravitation and electro-magnetism Yet to reconcile the contradictory ideas of action at a distance and continuous propagation has been the outstanding problem of physics ever since the days of Maxwell The picture of a swarm of discrete particles (presumably with all the classical properties of constant mass, simple location in space etc.) producing wave-like effects in their flight through space is an artificial devise It this is a picture of continuity in nature, as Sir Suleiman suggests, then, it is simply a restatement of the classical wave theory. What happens to action at a distance, then ? Besides, discontinuity is not really abolished in Sir Suleiman's picture, for, that is a picture of particles rushing through empty space All these difficulties (I have not stated them all) result from the refusal to abandon hypothetical concepts which have been exposed by experience as devoid of any ontological content The negative result of repeated experiment for finding velocity through ether does not leave any other alternative than to discard the idea of a stationary medium On the other hand, the breakdown of Bohr's model shows that the laws of classical mechanics can not be applied to the microcosmic world Here again, physics is forced to the conclusion that the electron must have a dual structure-it must be a "wavicle", to use the graphic term of Eddington From the point of view of classical absolutism, this may appear to be a "physical impossibility" But it becomes quite conceivable in the light of the empirical fact that mass is not a constant quantity. The decisive factor however is the equivalence of mass and energy - their identity. Conversion of the one to the other implies that somewhere in the process there must be a boundary condition, a transitional state representing an overlapping of the properties of particle and wave Groups of concentric waves appearing as particles, under certain conditions (Schroedinger's original hypothesis) do not present such an artificial picture as a swarm of particles producing wave-effects

From one side, physics has been compelled to abandon the idea of a medium of propagation, and, from the other, it has been pushed to the conclusion that matter ultimately is not a granular, but vibratory substance. Sir Suleiman seems to think that this is a paradoxical position. According to him, propagation of waves without a medium is a "physical impossibility" Is it, really? It may be, if waves are regarded as mere forms distinct from the substance For example, there can be no wave without water But are not the waves themselves parts of water? Is it very sensible or scientific to say that water is the medium of waves? Waves are nothing more than periodic changes in some substance. If they are regarded as forms, treated mathematically as magnitudes per se, the substance serves the purpose of medium But there are not two ontological entities. The relation is purely logical. The development of the undulatory theory of light led to this formalist conception of wave. It is rather too late to insist upon the superfluous notion of a medium

Schroedinger-waves are periodic changes in a vibratory substance - the so called field-scalar. It is the density of the electric charge of the field. Since the quantitative value of a charge of electricity is known, the physical magnitude of the groups of converging waves ("wave-packets") is a matter of differential calculus And it is found to be such as equates with the mass of electron So wave mechanics does not deny the reality of matter It deals with physical processes which cannot be analysed down to particles and propagation of energy through medium Quantum physics reduces matter to electricity which is vibratory as well as corpuscular. Static electricity (electric-field) is a field of vibratory motion An electric current is a stream of electrons which are material particles. As regards medium, the idea is utterly superfluous when we are dealing with an all-pervasive substance Just as in the theory of relativity space and time, as ontological categories, appear as functions of matter (mass), just so are the magnitudes of mass and energy traced down by quantum physics to the common foundation of a vibratory substance - action.

It has been suggested by positivist philosophers and some physicists, given illogically to super-empiricism, that these revolutionary discoveries about the nature of the foundation of the physical world make the concept of substance untenable Evidently, that is a verbal squibble The fact is that mass is no more absolute than space or time It is a relative concept The mass of a body is related to its motion The concept of substance has to be revised only in so far as it implied absoluteness of mass It is not composed of "rigid lumps of reality" But substance—the stuff of the world - remains , and the stuff of which the physical world is made is a material substance. Neither logically nor empirically, can the existence of matter be denied Philosophically, the reality of matter is guaranteed by the old principle —something cannot come out of nothing Even in the wildest philosophical mood, no physicist would dispute this principle Eddington falls back on the self-contradictory concept of "mind-stuff" there is something out of which the world is made, and that cannot be qualitatively different from the empirical constituents of physical things Denial of the reality of matter - a stuff that exists as a physical magnitude - logically leads to the fantastic view that the world of our experience is a fiction Therefore it is not possible for physics to deny the existence of matter without comitting suicide Sometimes ago, Einstein said that physicists like Eddington, Jeans and others did not themselves believe in what they preached, because why should they spend their lives gazing at distant stars, if they did not really believe in their existence ?

Apart from these logical and philosophical considerations, the fact remains that the Schroedinger Heisenberg theory of wave mechanics represents a new conception of matter Its constants are all physical entities Even Heisenberg, with his marked positivist bias, does not maintain that sub-atomic mechanism is not a physical process His is pure empiricism It may be mentioned that his mathematical apparatus (matrix-mechanics) is founded on Fourier's theorem. So, the physical principles of his new quantum theory are logically connected with the principles of classical mechanics He has shown it himself that they can be stated in Lagrangian and Hamiltonian equations His position is that it is useless for the purpose of exact measurement to assume motion (of revolving electron) that cannot be observed. In other words, spectral lines should not be explained by hypothetical processes inside the atoms ; the method should be reversed to infer various states of sub-atomic mechanism from spectroscopic phenomena that can be directly observed. If this positivist hyper-empiricism implies denial of the reality of matter, then, it is not a "heresy" of quantum physics. Barthelot, Mach, Ostwald and their followers took up a similar position as regards atom which, however, survived the bombardment of such heavy guns. The Heisenberg school rejects the Schroedinger idea of wave-packets on the ground that these are unobservable entities But here we have a difference of method only Because, Schroedinger was able to show that Heisenberg's theory led to the self same physical results. The radiation from atoms reveals their internal states, changes in which can be deduced from spectroscopic data Whatever may be the approach to the problem of sub-atomic mechanism, neither of the methods denies that the problem is physical, that the category (wave) mathematically or symbolically treated, is a physical magnitude - an ontological reality

It has been contended (by Eddington, Weyl and others) that Heisenberg's theory reduces substance to a mere logical concept, and inference from observed physical processes, that physics could leave that concept aside to deal formalistically only with the processes as periodic changes ; and that it is useless to raise the question - changes in what ? Because any answer will involve assumption of magnitudes not directly observable. Similar arguments were used by the Machians against the atomic hypothesis. They have no more force to-day than at that time. Leaving aside chemistry, the magnificient development of quantum physics proves that the atomic hypothesis was not useless

However, in short, the question raised by the new quantum theory is not about the ontological reality of microcosmic magnitude, it is about the usefulness (for technical scientific research) of assuming that they are magnitudes of something The suggestion of the Heisenberg school is that, instead of getting involved in a controversy about the structure of primordial matter, physics may, for its own purposes, deal with microcosmic phenomena symbolically Let us be content with measuring the measurable without bothering about the nature of magnitudes measured I need not go into the philosophy of this attitude which is logically fallacious The point is that it does not deny the existence of an object of measurement, and that is matter, however, may it be constructed.

As a matter of fact, philosophically, Heisenberg's position is Kantian. He suggests that, just as the theory of relativity compelled a profound revision of the traditional notions about space and time, quantum physics is bound to modify the concept of substance in the Kantian sense (vide "The Physical Principle of the Quantum Theory)". The ultimate object of knowledge is a formless mass which enters into our experience only when cast in certain a priori moulds of perception This fundamental principle of Kantian Epistemology is obviously quasi-subjectivist; but Kant was far from the absurd position of denying the reality of the object of knowledge. As a physicist, he was an orthodox Newtonian So, Heisenberg's inclination towards Kantian quasi-subjectivism does not imply denial of matter. He does not deny the objectivity of the material world. His point is that our knowledge of physical processes is largely subjective being necessarily dependent on our intelligence, there is a limit to the accuracy of measurement because in the microcosmic world the position and velocity of entities are disturbed by the very act of measuring them Evidently, the issue is epistemological - how far do physical theories, particularly those dealing with sub-miscroscopic processes, give a true picture of the objective reality? There is no question about the fundamental fact that physics does describe processes in something which actually exists - outside the mind of the physicists

A few words about the "waves of probability." It is not true that quantum physics regards matter as merely a bundle of such imaginary waves, as Sir Suleiman says The concept of probability has been introduced, not as regards matter itself, but to modify strict determinism If Born would regard Schroedinger's field-scalar as a "field of probability", that is purely for mathematical purposes For determining statistically at which point in a given field the centre of energy will appear, at a certain moment as the electron (particle), the physical nature of the field may be disregarded The desired result would be obtained by simply calculating the probabilities of the situation Mathematics is symbolism ; but it would have no sense, certainly no scientific value, if the symbols did not symbolise something The "field of probability" is the mathematical manner of saying that wherever certain conditions are given, the electron is highly probable to appear as a tangible physical entity.

Because of the experienced fact that there is a limit to the accuracy of calculation (for the present at any rate) microcosmic laws must be stated in terms of probability, though this may be so high as to amount to certainty Thus the introduction of the concept of probability does not mean that determinism is discarded Rejection of the idea of causality - that there are invariant relations in nature - will mean blasting the very foundations of science. For, the point of departure of all scientific enquiry is the belief that the universe is a law - governed system, and that these laws can be discovered and understood and quantitatively stated. Born himself has repudiated the neo-teleologist interpretation of Nernst, Riezler etc. of the concept of probability by declaring categorically that it would be entirely wrong to hold that the modification of the doctrine of causality revived the belief in miracles Indeed, except on the basis of causality, probability has no meaning How could we say that a certain event is probable to happen if we did not believe that it would take place as the effect of certain definite causes ? When these are few, the prediction is accurate to the extent of absolute certainty But the accuracy diminishes when a multitude of factors enter into the cause of an event The greater the multitude, the less the certainty of prediction But the uncertainty is never of such a magnitude as makes prediction impossible As long as predictions can be made, and events happen approximately as predicted, the principle of physical determinism stands The fact that under certain conditions, where individual entities cannot be abstracted from the multitude composed of them, prediction can be only statistical, does not change the position essentially The law of average is also a determinist law. Unless individual relations were causally determined, there would be no guarantee for the approximate accuracy of statistical predictions Statistically predicted events do happen approximately as predicted. That is the decisive proof, that at every stage, physical processes are causally determined Thus, it is vulgarisation of the mathematical technique suited to the peculiar problems of wave-mechanics, to say that this has reduced matter to a " bundle of the imaginary waves of probability A mathematical concept should not be confounded with a physical category

Any possible doubt about the reality of matter and causality disappears as soon as the empirically established physical principle of relativity is applied to the problems of quantum physics Rejection of the theory of relativity to-day would logically lead to the denial of the reality of matter, because mass is not an absolute category Absoluteness of time and reality of matter can no longer be defended together as the component elements of a logically self-contained system of objective knowledge One must go The former goes, the latter remains That's the finding of modern physics. It is a "heresy" in the same sense in which all new ideas were condemned heretical by the orthodox Heretics are the heralds of progress.

THE PHILOSOPHICAL REVOLUTION.

"We live in an age of science. Most people think that science has served humanity by producing electric light, motor cars, aeroplanes etc. That is only a partial view. In fact, few realise the outlook that science has produced during the last two hundred years. Science has given us a new view of the universe... . ..."

"The future of India depends on a courageous application of scientific knowledge. As man learns to apply the scientific method to the problems of every day life, in that measure he will rise to and reach his allotted height Let the dogs of conservatism, ignorance and fanaticism bark, but the glorious caravan of the Indian nation will move on with irresistible force".— Sir C. V. Raman,

(At the Convocation of the University of Bombay, 1932)

How many of the graduates - the trusted and sanguine custodians of India's future - fully grasped the revolutionary implication of the momentous utterance ? Lest it should be drowned in the din of doubtful wisdom and platitudinous preachings that fill the intellectual atmosphere of our country, the progressive youth might profitably remember, and reflect upon the weighty utterance of the distinguished savant

One of the greatest scientists of our days, very creditably for himself, advocates a philosophical revolution as the condition for the much delayed, but inevitable, national Renaissance of India The adoption of a scientific outlook, the application of the scientific method to the problems of life, will necessarily mean the rejection of ideas, ideals, 'institutions and traditions which are erroneously cherished as the peculiar features of Indian culture and to preserve and glorify which has consequently become an article of faith of Indian Nationalism. The posture of standing with the face turned backward is obviously incompatible with any striving for progress The method and point of departure must be changed before any advance is possible

Scientific outlook is essentially materialistic - a term so very misunderstood and piously abhorred generally in India. At any rate, scientific outlook is free from preconceived notions. It does not take anything for granted It does not admit miracles occasional or perpetual It seeks and eventually finds, the cause of every phenomenon in order to understand that particular phenomenon and its connection with others Whenever an event or appearance happens to defy understanding, and seems to disregard or transcend all the known laws of nature, the scientific mind does not call in the aid of prejudice and superstition It simply admits its inability to comprehend the cause of the apparent miracle, but with the firm conviction that diligent and dispassionate investigation will, sooner or later, unravel what for the moment appears to be a mystery Empirically established laws of nature are never suspended to make manifest supernatural powers In short, scientific outlook does not admit of the possibility of something coming out of nothing There is a causal connection in the interminable chain of events Scientific mind rejects the theological maxim - "Ex nihili omnium" in favour of the thesis of the ancient Greeks "Ex nihili nihil" Scientific outlook is based on positive knowledge, not on belief, speculation or fantasy As such, it is hostile to the religious, metaphysical, teleological view of the Universe, life, history and society. This view is opposed to all free enquiry. Its pivot is authority which defies or eludes test It declares human knowledge not only imperfect, but unreliable, placing it within insurmountable bounds.

Scientific method is inductive - to reach the general from the particular, the abstract from the concrete, the unknown from the known The spiritual view of life follows in contrast the deductive method - to start from an assumption, a hypothesis, which can never be verified, to explain phenomena in the light (?) of an unknown and unknowable noumenon

The religious, metaphysical, teleological view of life - a view that arrogates the pious distinction of spiritualism and starts from an assumption or unverifiable hypothesis, a Divine Providence, Cosmic Will, First Principle or Final Cause - is not a special genius of India It dominates the life of every man, every where, until the sublime light of science dawns upon him, and dissipates the mist of ignorance, prejudice and superstition that has previously clouded his understanding As long as he is not able to explain the multitudinous phenomena of nature that surround, surprise and often terrify him, he rather helplessly than piously attributes their cause to some providential agency. Since his own life is actuated by motives, he imagines a Cosmic Will behind the natural phenomena which appear to be so well adapted and regulated for his benefit. Inside and outside himself, man finds an infinite variety of things advantageous to himself. for example. his physical organs and mental capacities, as well as the sun, air, water etc. These useful things have been made neither by himself nor by any other man before. So, there must be a final cause for them all. The unscientific mind can not conceive of such well regulated things happening by themselves, without a plan made and directed by an intelligent force, which by its very nature must be omnipotent, omnipresent and omniscient He never stops to ask how did the final cause come into being. That would be irreligious

Thus assumed by the ignorance of man, the hypothetical being (which might pass under any of the various denominations - God, Universal Soul, Divine Providence, First Principle, Final Cause etc.) becomes the supreme object and the inexhaustible source of all knowledge Intellectual and spiritual activity of man becomes a long, dismal search for a light which always recedes before any approach, luring the unfortunate votary into a confusion, confounded progressively by the vanity of virtue But there have been candid souls who would rather admit defeat than seek the questionable glory of self-deception or fraudulent victory For instance, the venerable Roman philosopher, Seneca, pathetically declared that the longer he contemplated Plato's sublime conception of the Triad (the First Cause, the Logos and the

Universal Soul), the less he could grasp of it In such vain pursuit, philosophy degenerates into a dreary record of endless dispute, or pedantic dissertations about the nature of an hypothetical being which must always remain a hypothesis, since it could never be verified by the vulgar, but the only reliable, test of experience.

Ideas, ideals, institutions and traditions, that are fondly cherished as the token of the supposed superiority of India's culture, belong to the dark ages of humanity, when prejudice parades in the garb of piety, ignorance claims the sublimity of virtue, and idle speculation puts on the dignity of philosophy The spell is broken ultimately by the first conquests of science.

The epoch-making discoveries of Galileo, Copernicus and Kepler shattered the foundation of the time-honoured religious philosophy, and the metaphysical outlook of Universe and life It was found that observation of natural phenomena without any preconceived notion led to conclusions which upset the celestial and terrestrial order sanctioned by religion and theology. A philosophical revolution took place. A radical change in the outlook on the problems of the Universe, life, history and society became inevitable. That change was a condition for the great political revolutions of the seventeenth and eighteenth centuries which ushered in the marvellous era of modern civilisation

The definite inauguration of a new philosophy on the basis of experimental science and the inductive method of reasoning, is associated with the names of Francis Bacon and Descartes. It will be interesting and instructive to recollect Bacon's characterisation of the old orthodox method that he set out to combat, and enunciation of the new he advocated "Whence can arise such vagueness and sterility in all the physical systems which have hitherto existed in the world? It is not certainly from anything in nature itself, for the steadiness and regularity of the laws by which it is governed clearly mark them out as objects of certain and precise knowledge It can therefore arise from nothing else but the perverseness and insufficiency of the methods which have been pursued. Men have sought to make the world from their own conception, and to draw from their own minds all the materials which they employed; but if, instead of doing so, they had consulted experience and observation, they would have had facts, and not opinions, to reason about, and might have ultimately arrived at the knowledge of the laws which govern the material world. As things are at present conducted, a sudden transition is made from sensible objects and particular facts, to general propositions which are accepted principles, and round which, as round so many fixed poles, disputations and arguments continually revolve From the propositions thus hastily assumed, all things are derived by a process compendious and precipitate, ill suited to discovery, but wonderfully accommodated to debate The way that promises success is the reverse of this. It requires that we should generalise slowly, going from particular things to those that are but one step more general, from those to others of still greater extent, and soon to such as are universal. By such means we may hope to arrive at principles, not vague and obscure, but luminous and well-defined, such as nature herself will not refuse to accept. I propose to establish progressive stages of certainty The evidence of sense, helped and guarded by a certain process of correction, I retain ; but the mental operation which follows the act of sense, I, for the most part reject and instead of it, I open and lay out a new and certain path for the mind to proceed in, starting directly from the simple sensuous perceptions.

With all his brilliance, Bacon, however, felt his unexplored way with caution and prudence He avoided a frontal attack upon the established creeds and institutions of religion, while dexterously shaking its very foundation. He adopted a clever stratagem. He did not deny the existence of God or the immortality of the soul, but pleaded that these basic questions of faith should be answered by philosophy instead of by theology; that is to say, by reason instead of by dogma Once God and soul are placed under the step-motherly care of philosophy, nothing but dire misfortune can overtake these venerable prejudices You can just as well take a fish out of water and let it thrive on the high and dry land. Disguised as an humble faithful, the infidel threw down the fateful gauntlet to the faith together with her shady entourage of teleology, theology and metaphysics which had for ages served as so many fetters for the spirit of man The war thus declared over three hundred years ago, is still being waged. Science has scored splendid victories, but she had to fight every inch of the ground. With desperate tenacity prejudice had resisted its advancing opponent, and the final victory of science is still to be won.

Descartes opened the attack more courageously than his older contemporary. His starting point was absolute doubt about everything the reality and veracity of which could not be established by sense perception The rejection of authority as the unquestionable testimony for truth logically led to the deposition of theology from the proud position it had occupied for more than a thousand years Nothing should be accepted as true unless it were proved to be so, and the standard of truth was not authority or the mystic fantasy called revelation, but reason. In expounding his memorable theory of vortices, Descartes, indeed, made a concession to the time-honoured prejudice regarding the origin of creation; but the sheer formality of his accommodating attitude was unmistakably exposed by the cynical remark that "yet it would be of eminent interest to see how the Universe might have evolved by itself" In the bloody age of heresy hunting, the very postulation of such a hypothesis represented great boldness which could proceed only from a firm scientific conviction The Cartesian theory of vortices marks the beginning of modern physics and cosmology. It was the continuation of ancient atomism, propounded by the philosophers of ancient Greece,—Democritos and Epicuros, the brilliant light of knowledge which had been all but extinguished in the dark ages of religiosity, miracles and revealed wisdom. Since the days of Descartes, physics has advanced with giant strides, pushing aside his ingenious hypothesis which, nevertheless, will always retain the great merit of having boldly blazed the trail of progress - of inaugurating a new era of spiritual freedom The great merit of the Cartesian hypothesis was that it constructed a physical system in which the forced assumption of an original creator appeared to be entirely superfluous, the process of the evolution of the Universe being purely mechanical, the creator having absolutely no power to alter the minutest detail

Both the founders of the scientific method emphatically repudiated the prejudice of a Final Cause In view of this decisive negative attitude regarding the cardinal principle of religion and theology, their forced and formal recognition of the existence of God loses the cogency of conviction Descartes wrote "we can only presume it (the first creation by god), since God did not take us into his counsel " This habit of searching for a Final Cause has no use for the knowledge of physical and natural things. In physics, the appeal to a Final Cause is idle, since every conclusion must rest on solid ground "

The philosophical revolution heralded by Bacon and Descartes triumphantly marched ahead during the last three hundred years. With its iconoclastic methods, science advanced steadily, showing how flagrantly the certainties of experience contradicted, and were contradicted by, the notions and fantasies which had been raised on the proud pedestal of eternal truth by authority and superstition. Time-honoured articles of faith, teleological explanation of the problems of nature and society, the misty wisdom of metaphysics - all these landmarks of the spiritualist view of life could not stand the test of inductive enquiry. It became evident that should the old mode of thought remain in force, should established doctrines, dogmas and authority continue to govern the life of man, individually and socially, his own experience must be disbelieved, knowledge must be fearfully shunned as the serpent in the garden of Eden, superstition must be cherished as spirituality, ignorance adored as virtue, vain fantasy accorded the distinction of revealed wisdom, and we should still appeal to Popes and priests for the answer to the problems of the physical and social sciences But the imperious advance of knowledge enabled man to withdraw more and more phenomena from the inscrutable will of supernatural agencies, and trace their causes to immanent properties and mechanical laws of nature

Still, whenever and wherever science failed to give fully satisfactory explantion of all the phenomena, man continued to place reliance upon supernatural agencies supposing them to be beyond the reach of science and maintaining in consequence that the defective and imperfect scientific knowledge, which could never attain the absolute truth, was itself possible only owing to the "divine spark" in man. The inscrutable will and invisible hand of the Almighty were triumphantly detected whenever the mechanical laws of nature were not yet discovered or the operation of them appeared to be suspended by the intervention of unforeseen factors Ignorance became the shrine of God, the only argument in favour of religion Hence there were men, with a completely scientific out look in astronomical, physical and chemical method in the investigation of the organic world, particularly in human affairs Biology and psychology still remained confused by theological and metaphysical prejudices

It is, however, no paradox that so many scientifically minded men, even some great scientists themselves, should linger undert he waning influence of religion and metaphysics. The cause of the apparent paradox was the specialisation of scientific study. Scientists had to devote themselves wholly to particular branches of investigation. Consequently, their vision was circumscribed by the happenings in small limited fields which were but minute fractions of the vast domaine of the Universe. Sole occupation with particular groups of phenomena made the average man of science lose sight of the comprehensive nature of scientific knowledge as a whole. As it were, they fail to see the forest for the trees. The very creditable and profusely productive zeal for practice in detail eclipsed the broad vision of theory. In short, many scientists were not able to draw general philosophical consequences from their own discoveries and knowledge. The co-ordination of the vast knowledge, acquired in the diverse branches of science, was left to philosophy. But to perform that function, philosophy had to revolutionise herself.

The development of biology quickened the philosophical revolution. All animals lower than man had been characterised by Descartes as automata. The discovery that organisms were also governed by mechanical laws enabled the French philosopher de la Metrie to shock the prejudiced world by declaring that man was also a machine. Comparative anatomy traced the descent of man from lower forms of animals; and all the diverse phenomena of the organic world were reduced to a common point of origin which merged into the primordial unity of inorganic matter. The mysterious entity life was discovered to be nothing but a property of organic matter. Ideas were proved to be the production of mind, which in its turn is a function of a material organ, the brain. In consequence of all these revolutionary discoveries regarding the mysterious vital phenomena as well as the so-called spiritual essence of man, the old conception of soul - the immortal divine spark in man - appeared to be only an imagination With its individual expression, the universal soul must also go

While each great discovery of science dealt a staggering blow to the hoary castle of religion, built in the air of faith, and consequently added stone after stone to the solid foundation of the philosophy of Materialism, prejudice persisted by virtue of momentum. In course of time, the progress of the philosophical revolution was retarded by the change in the social position of the bourgeoisie Struggling to liberate themselves from feudal bondage, the bourgeoisie had found a powerful weapon inthe revolutionary philosophical consequences of science By repudiating the authority of religion and theology, science destroyed the ideological foundation and moral justification of the feudal social order. The bourgeoisie preached and practised the "sacred right of revolt" in temporal as well as in spiritual matters, and became the ruling power. In a changed situation, advantageous to themselves, their philosophical outlook changed As an oppressed class, they had advocated revolution, ideological as well as political In power, they became conservative Without authority, there could be no domination of one class over the entire society, an authority on earth could not be firmly established unless backed, directly or indirectly, by some supernatural sanction So, faith and religion were rescued from their ruins For the vulgar, the old discredited God with all his threadbare paraphernalia, was again allowed to rule, the intellectual elite, however, had become too sophisticated to relapse into crude belief, severely shaken, if not thoroughly exploded, by science For their edification, religion appeared in the new garb of modern idealist philosophy. The untenable doctrine of a personal creator was replaced by the fascinating fantasy of the Absolute Idea The bitterest critic of the Christian Church, the cynical Voltaire, himself became an advocate of the lost cause, and replied the atheism of the philosopher Pierre Bayle with the following argument "If there is no God, we must discover one Give Bayle five hundred peasants to rule, and he will immediately recognise the usefulness of religion" That was the most forceful argument against the case in the defense of which it was advanced It showed up God and religion in their true role A few decades later, Kant did not blush to proclaim that he must set aside science in order to make room for faith. Yet, his "all-shattering" critical philosophy has swept away all the debris of medieval speculation His monumental work on the theory of Newton had driven

God even away from the precarious position conceded by the latter.

If the selfish interest of the bourgeoisie came in conflict with the philosophical revolution, and sought to curbe its progress, the future of mankind required its culmination. Therefore it was impossible to resist the historical striving for the proper appreciation of the far-reaching theoretical value of scientific discoveries in their entirety with the object of weaving them into a comprehensive system of philosophy To disown the materialist tendency of its birth, modern philosophy launched upon the wild career of idealism which was raised to a giddy height by Hegel In his eagerness to vindicate the basic principle of true philosophy, - the primal unity of things - Hegel destroyed modern classical Idealism Without a dualist conception of the Universe - matter and spirit - idealist philosophy is not possible The monist conception must be either materialist, or be lost in the inextricable wilderness of solipsism or nihilism If the original unity is reduced to a spiritual existence, the phenomenal world must be declared to be a hallucination For, matter can never evolve out of pure spirit, except with the intervention of omnipotence which knows no law With the postulate of such intervention, religion is restored to the throne of authority, and philosophy must accept a humble place at the foot of the throne Besides, spirit itself cannot exist without being subordinated to the limitation of space, in which case it would cease to be what it claims to be. Since in the age of science and positive knowledge mankind cannot possibly believe that the grand process of the evolution of the Universe is a bad dream, Materialism must be its philosophy, should it have any philosophy worth the name.

In the middle of the nineteenth century, the lowered banner of philosophical revolution was raised again, this time by the ideologists of the toiling masses. The new leaders of the revolution were equipped with a formidable weapon forged by the latest and the greatest idealist philosopher, Hegel It was the dialectic method of thought which ousted formal logic Exposing the transitoriness of everything, and revealing the constant conception of a new in the womb of the passing old, dialectics put an end to all authority. No weapon could be more welcome to the leaders of the philosophical revolution Out of the magnificent ruins of Hegelian Absolute Idealism, Feuerbach rescued the positive contribution of the classical philosophy as the basis of the "Philosophy of the Future" - Materialism. Armed with an encyclopedic knowledge of all the sciences, Karl Marx and Friedrich Engels clearly and comprehensively stated the new outlook of life, opened by the discoveries of science during the preceding three hundred years In the bright light of that materialist outlook, all the problems of nature, life, history and society, appears devoid of all mystery, and man attains the full height of his glory as the sole master of his fate

Undoubtedly, even to-day, science has not penetrated into all the mysteries of the Universe But what has been conclusively established is the certainty of scientific knowledge, and that there is nothing unknowable Our knowledge is not perfect - far from being so , but there is no limit to our capacity to know. Besides, perfect knowledge is an ideal, never to be attained, because when there will be nothing more to know, extinction will overtake mankind Science has burst the bubble of absolute knowledge and eternal truth Everyday we know more, consequently, our knowledge is constantly rectified, enlarged and amplified The summum bonum of scientific knowledge is that there is nothing fixed-everything is in a constant flux The only thing eternal and immutable is perpetual change, and that this eternal phenomenon of change is governed by mechanical laws inherent in itself Thus science justifies its name by merging itself into philosophy, and philosophy ceases to be idle and vain speculation to stand out in the fullness of the glory of the science of sciences

RELIGION AND SUPERSTITION

In a statement made at the termination of his fast, Mahatma Gandhi expressed the following optimistic view. "The tremendous awakening that has taken place in the country during these five days fills me with a hope that orthodoxy will surpass itself and rid Hinduism of the canker of untouchability which is eating into its vitals." At the same time, he declared: "I could not expect all of a sudden to revolutionise Hindu thought." One may be surprised to hear two such discordant notes struck simultaneously. But a little reflection reveals that the pessimistic note which, by the way, is more in tune with the rude realities of the situation, flows logically from the fallacious basis of the Mahatma's optimism. He hopes that the easy success of his threat to put on the crown of martyrdom will induce Hindu orthodoxy to give up voluntarily a prejudice which is so very essential for its very existence. Orthodoxy must cease to be itself if it were to perform what the Mahatma's stout optimism expects of it. What is expected is nothing short of suicide. As such, vicarious offerings are seldom made in this world of realities, the Mahatma has ample reason to be pessimistic on afterthought.

A thorough revolutionisation of Hindu thought is, indeed, the condition for the removal of untouchability together with many other social evils which hamper India's social progress. But this condition can never be fulfilled with the sanction of those very elements which will be destroyed by the revolution. Revolutionisation of Hindu thought means nothing less than the end of Hindu orthodoxy, of the Hindu religion itself. Superstition and prejudice are the twin pillars on which all religions rest. Remove these props, and the entire venerable edifice of religion collapses. This general rule is all the more applicable to Hinduism which is reared rather upon social customs and habits than upon an established form of worship or a uniform system of theological dogmas supporting certain definite articles of faith. Curiously enough, those who call themselves "aggressive nationalists" base the claim to superiority for Hinduism precisely on this evidence of its backwardness Even as a religion, Hinduism bears the stamp of backwardness. Rigorous mono-theism is the highest form of religion.

The essence of all religion is the belief in one or more supernatural forces (personified or in abstract) exercising control or dominion over things and events terrestrial As soon as man thus resigns his being and will to the inviolable guardianship of an agency, the existence and power of which are assumed apriori he naturally sacrifices reason on the alter of superstition, he barters away his native claim to knowledge for the complacence of prejudices which derive the force of venerable wisdom and divine truth from fraudulent practices. The primitive inquisitiveness gives way to the awe or wonder for powers supernatural, never to be comprehended by human mind Criticism makes room for credulity Ignorance becomes bliss, and proudly insults the search for truth as vain and delusive.

These evidences of "spiritualist genius" are not the monopoly of India. They fill the history of all religions. For example, Tertullian, one of the fathers of the Christian church, asserted that the problem that had occupied the great philosophers of Greece were no problem for an ordinary Christian artisan.

Similarly, to-day, any Hindu pseudo-intellectual would readily repeat the cheap sneer of Swami Vivekanand that Hindu philosophy begins where Western knowledge ends Prejudice confounds theology with philosophy, - with an impatient gesture of supposed superiority Even the intelligent do not notice that their specious arguments against the reliability of scientific knowledge only reveals the damaging fact that ignorance is the foundation of religion - that God can dwell only in darkness

Yet, religion represents the ideology of human society at a certain stage of its evolution Essentially based upon ignorance - superstition and prejudice - religion nevertheless is not a constant phenomenon Like all social phenomena, it changes constantly Its forms change together with (under the influence of) the changes in the material conditions of social life The religion of a people, therefore, is a reliable measure of its social progress It is the gauge of its civilisation.

The religion of primitive peoples takes the form of fetichism - the worship of stones, trees, animals and crudely constructed idols. Gradual development of the faculty of imagination creates the belief in a variety of gods, 'as so many personifications of natural phenomena the cause of which are unknown to the primitive man In its earlier stage, the belief in supernatural forces and beings is the product of awe caused by incomprehensible events, such as thunder, lightning, earthquake, flood, draught, pestilence etc etc Fear is the most fertile breeding ground of superstition Worship takes the form of sacrifice to propitiate the gods Those officiating at the sacrificial ceremonies gradually grow up into a caste of priests, claiming the occult power to know the devious ways and inscrutable wills of the gods By virtue of its office, and thanks to the prevalence of superstition the sacerdotal caste becomes all-powerful To increase and consolidate its power, the priestly caste promotes superstitious practices so as to raise them to the noble status of social virtue - the evidence of religiosity. The priests can propitiate the angry gods, or secure boons from the milder and indulgent ones They are supposed to be in the possession of occult wisdom which makes them conversant with the ways of the gods who govern the destiny of mankind, - ways that are not to be comprehended by the ordinary mortal Consequently, the word of the priest becomes the law of society. The supremacy of the priest is guaranteed by an elaborate system of traditions, customs, institutions and ceremonies, superstitious observance of which establishes the distinction of proud orthodoxy meritorious religiosity.

Intellectual progress enables man eventually to rise above the savagery of fetichism, and, later, above polytheistic beliefs. The worship of stones, trees and animals no longer affords him sufficient spiritual satisfaction which he needs as the only solace in the dark and distressing perspective of the chaos created by the dissolution of the primitive tribal society The disintegration of the tribal and patriarchal social order inevitably shakes the belief in its patron deities and their sacerdotal ministers Advance of knowledge undermines the foundation of gross superstition The power and position of priesthood are challenged by the growing desire to enquire into the nature of things The desire culminates in the erection of the glorious monument of the ancient materialistic and speculative philosophies

But positive knowledge is still too backward to overwhelm superstition It leaves the masses unaffected A new form of religion arises on a subtle basis which fortifies faith by purging it of fetichistic and polytheistic crudities. Monotheistic religions claim Divine Revelation for their origin. Superstition acquires new strength For, the dogma of revelation must be established by miracles which suspending the laws of nature makes the will of God manifest. Popular credulity makes history out of imaginary legends, and fraudulent practices serve the holy purpose Laws of nature are the manifestation of the will of God; yet these very laws must be suspended to make the will of God manifest to the vulgar eye Such a flagrantly illogical and self-contradictory doctrine must be rejected as fantastic and absurd or accepted as divine, inspired, revealed wisdom, since no human mind could possibly have conceived it. Under the new religion, human life continues to be guided, though no longer by a number of discredited deities, yet by the inscrutable will of a supreme being or the mysterious operation of some supernatural force

Monotheism represents the striving for the establishment of a centralised society on the ruins of the antic order of warring city states or inflated empires - conglomerations of heterogeneous peoples held together by brute force As such, it attacks all the ceremonies, customs, traditions, institutions, and habits established by the earlier form of religion. Barbarous prejudices descending from the days of fetichism are replaced by the dogmas of theology. The poetic idolatry of polytheistic superstition gives way to the blind faith in a supreme being or the mystic notion of an inexplicable first principle.

But dogmatic theology, futile speculations about the nature of the unknown and unknowable final cause, and the vain efforts for the realisation of the unrealisable - all these start as much from preconceived notions and superstitious beliefs as the fearful worship of fetichism or the devout ceremonies of natural religion Monotheistic religions free human mind from the bondage of grosser superstition, while encumbering it with more subtle forms of the same virtue or vice which, nevertheless, are not altogether incompatible with social progress Indeed, under certain conditions of history, monotheistic religion is the ideology of the forces of social revolution The monotheism of Jesus Christ and later on of Mohammed laid down the foundation of modern European culture

Vedic Hinduism was a natural religion In course of time, its social basis - clan and patriarchal family - decayed The decomposition appears to have reached the climax towards the end of the Epic Era when the Kshatriya clans were practically all exterminated in a gigantic civil war, depicted in the Mahabharata But there did not emerge from the chaos any force of a new cohesion. Brahmanic supremacy became absolute in the conditions of social dissolution The natural religion of the Vedas, instead of being replaced by a higher form of faith, namely, monotheism degenerated into the fatalism of the

Smritis and the absurd extravagances of Puranic superstitions. Eventually, the quasi-materialistic agnosticism of Buddha spread as the ideology of a great social revolution which was to clear away the ruins of the antique society But sacerdotal tyranny of the Brahmans had been entrenched behind superstitions, ceremonies and customs which defied reform on the authority of the Vedas, always true and infallible because of their supposed divine origin This doctrine concerning the origin of the Vedas was very useful for fraudulent practices Brahmanic absolutism was continuously reinforced by opportune interpolations. Supported by the insidiously fostered forces of popular superstition, Hindu orthodoxy resisted the triumphant march of the Buddhist revolution for nearly a thousand years, and finally overwhelmed it That was the most tragic event in the history of India The cause of the defeat of Buddhism was that it was rather nihilistic than monotheistic On the other hand, the rudiment of materialism inherent in a religion making no place for God, was not boldly developed Consequently, Buddhism went down in the morass of monastic absurdities and extravagances, and was eventually contaminated by the very corruptions it had revolted against.

Victorious Hindu reaction, while arming itself with Sankaracharya's ambiguous monotheism, could consolidate its shaken position only by fomenting the forces of popular ignorance and superstition. The ceremonies and worships of the Vedic religion had been greatly suppressed during the Buddhist period. Whatever still survived, was condemned by Sankar's reform. But Hindu theology, either of the pre-Buddhist era or of Sankar, remained a monopoly of the Brahman intellectual, and monastic orders. The masses of the people were left without any religion except the superstitions of the degenerate Pauranic faith, and a rich store of social prejudices (caste, untouchability, bichar) jealously guarded and persistently fostered by Brahmanic orthodoxy.

To-day, after the lapse of many hundreds of years, the religious life of the masses of the Hindu population is little changed. It is devoid of any spiritual ardour, being a dull monotony of superstitious customs and habits. The ordinary member of the Hindu society is without any definite creed or faith; his idea of God is hazy, he seldom performs any devotional practice regularly, as a matter of fact, he is a remarkably irreligious man. But his orthodoxy flames into fanaticism with regard to the prejudices and superstitions governing his daily life. He blindly believes in the law of karma which, if logically interpreted, must dispense with the doctrine of a supernatural force guiding human life Still, he has been taught through ages that this inexorable law is the expression of the inflexible will of God, which can be propitiated only through the scrupulous respect for traditional social customs, and rigid practice of bichar in personal habits. The pernicious doctrine of karma sanctifies all the inequities and inequalities of the Hindu society. Social tyranny and ostracism receive the stamp of divine justice - the fate of everybody has been determined by his own karma in a previous birth It is a vicious circle, with no way for escape The superstitious belief in the doctrine of karma kills all initiative in an orthodox Hindu His religion is to observe patiently and passively an absurd mass of time - honoured customs and rights

In the light of this hastily drawn sketch of the the historical background of Hindu society, the problem of untouchability takes on a more serious aspect than can be abolished with the magnanimous sanction of orthodoxy. It is an integral part of a whole complex of problems. Therefore it can not be solved separated from the complex which is the fossilised Hindu society. It is a ludicrous superstition, but exactly as such it is the pillar of Hindu orthodoxy. Untouchability and the allied social curses will go only with Hindu orthodoxy itself, which instituted them to reinforce the undermined foundation of its holy temple. You cannot preserve the temple as an eternal monument, and clear away the debris which serve the purpose of its foundation Those who devoutly worship in the sepulchral temple of Hindu orthodoxy, therefore, cannot afford to tinker with its decayed foundation, since that would bring the precarious edifice crashing down upon their heads. At best, they may try to embellish the ugly ruin with superficial patchwork

Untouchability will go only when the multitudinous victims of Hindu orthodoxy will outgrow the sinister spell of superstition Hindu society and Hindu thought will be revolutionised not by the martyrdom of a Mahatma It will be done by irresistible assaults upon the holy rampart of superstition sanctified with the name of religion These assaults are being delivered even to-day by the inexorable forces of economic necessity which do not obey the law of karma Theatrical demonstrations of liberalism on the part of orthodox caste-Hindus are but faint echos of the thunder of the impending revolution, they are rather feeble and futile efforts to ward off the nemesis of orthodoxy.

THE CULT OF ASCETICISM AND RENUNCIATION

I SOCIAL DISEASE

The National Renaissance of any people has for one of its conditions a critical view not only of the given epoch, but of its entire history For the present is but a product of the past A thorough change of the conditions of any given period requires, first of all, the discovery of the causes of those conditions which are usually rooted even in the remotest past of its history An unbroken causal chain connects historical events which superficially might appear not only disconnected, but positively chaotic The present conditions of India, for example, are considered to be the result of foreign rule To stop there is to tell only half the truth What was the cause of the foreign conquest? That could not be an historical phenomenon without cause The cause of that event must be sought in the past history of the Indian people Some social disease must have enervated it so as to become an easy prey of foreign invaders In short, only a critical examination of the past enables a people to discover the root cause of its present conditions, and the change of these latter depends upon the eradication of the former

So long as a people seeks the consolation for its present misery in the real or imaginary glory of the past, the doors of the future remain closed before it Glorification of the past is a prominent characteristic of Indian Nationalism Critical study of our own history is foreign to its ideology Drunk with the cheap satisfaction that Indian culture, being "spiritual", is superior to that of other people, we do not think that there is anything for us to learn from the history of foreign countries Otherwise, it would be evident that "the special features" of Indian culture also marked the history of the peoples In the critical history of other peoples we might find a picture of our own past and be impelled to discover in our own history similar causes that produced analogous phenomena in other countries It is generally believed that renunciation of the world in quest of a spiritual life is the badge of superiority of Indian culture When the same practice is found to have been rampant also in other countries, India must give up her claim to distinction at least on that score The favourite theory of our past thus shaken, there must begin a critical study of history as the necessary condition for the conquest of the future

"The (early Christian) ascetics were inspired by the savage enthusiasm which represents man as a criminal and God as a tyrant " (Gibbon, The Decline and Fall of the Roman Empire) The ascetic Christians as distinguished from the "vulgar" renounced all the pleasures of life and duties of society They lived on coarse and scanty food, begged or voluntarily offered Their food excluded meat, and drink excluded wine They practised celebacy No marriage was allowed Body and mind were mortified by all sorts of cruel device Natural inclinations of body as wes as of mind (love, affection, cheerfulness, rest, recreation etc) were condemned as vices Monasticism was rampant Thousands and thousands of "ascetics fled from a orofane and degenerate world to prepetual solitude or religious society They resigned the use or the property of their temporal possessions...... They soon acquired the respect of the world which they despised; and loudest adplause was bestowed on their divine philosophy which suppressed, without the aid of science or reason, the laborious virtues of the Grecian schools". (Ibid)

A critical historian would have the courage to depict a similar picture of the ancient and mediaeval India Not only that is done, but similar practices are still extolled as highly commendable with sublime indifference to science and reason.

Not only did Christianity preach asceticism and renunciation of the world as virtues Previously, the Pythagoreans had practised silence and submission as the gates of wisdom With the Stoics also the contempt of fortune, pain and death was the badge of a philosopher, and the Cynics had demonstrated their disdain for the amenities of life and the established customs of society

As the Pro-Consul of the Asiatic provinces of the Roman Republic, the philosophic Pliny was amused and astonished to find (in the early years of the Christian era) " solitary people who subsisted without money, who propagated without women (that is, whose number increased by the influx of new proselytes), and who derived from the disgust of mankind a perpetual supply of voluntary associates." ("Natural History")

Asceticism had been practised by the Jewish Prophets during many hundred years before the rise of Christianity. John the Baptist was the last of a long succession of Prophets who shunned the world and thundered anathema against its vices, allurements, futility and transitoriness. The rise of Christianity was immediately preceded by the appearance of a numerous Jewish sect (the Essenians) who adopted the creed of asceticism. Then there were the Gnostics, and the mystic votaries of Alexandrian Neo-Platonism. All were so many symptoms of a social crisis which appeared to be insurmountable Christian monasticism was the acute state of that social disease The Christian monks only went farther than their pagan ancestors "The votaries of divine philosophy aspired to imitate a purer and more perfect model. They trod in the footsteps of the prophets who had retired to the deserts; and they resorted to the devout and contemplative life which had been instituted by the Essenians in Palestine and Egypt.' (Gibbon, Ibid)

The beginning of Christian monasticism can be traced to Egypt, aptly characterised by Gibbon as "the fruitful parent of superstition". An illiterate youth named Anthony was the pioneer of the cult. He gave up his patrimony, deserted his family and retired to the desert where he devoted himself to a life of meditation and prayer accompanied by self-mortification with fanatical rigour The destitute Egyptian peasant soon became famous as the torch-bearer of divine light His example was followed by thousands. In the beginning, the Christian Church looked askance at the monastic movement But the genius of Athanasius - the redoubtable father of Catholic orthodoxy - had the courage to face the fact Anthony became a Saint, and the powerful Bishop understood that the Church must reconcile herself with, and patronise, a movement which was striking its roots deep into the spiritual imagination of the destitute masses Later on, under the protection and patronage of the powerful Catholic Church, monasteries stood out as flourishing islands in the desolate sea of the social ruin that followed the fall of the Roman Empire Religious discipline, superstition of holy severity - was the impetus to the voluntary labour of the monks which replaced the disrupted old means of production, namely, slavery

The prolific colonies of monks multiplied in the deserts of Lybia, on the rocks of the Thebias, and in the cities throughout the valley of the Nile. The mountains and deserts in the very neighbourhood of the Egyptian capital were crowded with monks. No less than fifty monasteries were established by Anthony and his disciples. The ruins of those monuments of monasticism are still present for the observation of curious travellers. The monastic order of Anthony was composed of isolated individuals given to a life of penance, prayer and meditation, in the solitude of the desert and mountains.

Pachonius established "organised communities" of recluses. "Brothers" thus living together were subjected to a severe and rigid system of the rules of conduct. Thus rose the monasteries which played such an important economic role to rescue society from the ruins of the Roman Empire. The first monastery of the Pachonian Order, founded on a small desolate island in the Upper Nile, was peopled by fourteen hundred brethren. In quick succession the holy abbott established nine such communities for men and one also for women. Very soon the number embraced no less than fifty thousand members, pledged to strict celebacy, rigorous asceticism, severe mortification of body and mind, and complete indifference to the enjoyments of worldly life. That numerous order of devout fanatics was held together by "the Angelic rules of discipline" framed by the founder.

The populace and once prosperous cities of the lower Nile were often crowded with thousands of males and females belonging to the monastic profession. Since the temples could not accomodate the credulous crowd of devotees, public edifices and even the city walls were used as pulpits and places of worship According to the historian Rufinus, once upon a time half the entire population of Egypt had taken to the holy life of asceticism either as recluses in the solitude, or under the "Angelic discipline" of monasticism Gibbon writes that in those days "in Egypt it was less difficult to find a God than a man"

The knowledge and the practice of the holy life of asceticism were introduced into Rome by Athanasius. The disciples of Anthony founded a settlement in the "capital of the world" Gibbon writes "The strange and savage appearance of these Egyptians excited, at first, horror and contempt, and, at length, applause and jealous imitation The Senators, and more specially the matrons, transformed their palaces and villas into religious houses" The apparent homage to the new institution of piety and devotion was rather an interest for a novelty which amused the jaded life of idleness and luxury, than a sign of spiritual fervour Fear also played its role to enshrine the new superstition in the place of the old pagan prejudice Encouragement to the holy institution was expected to be recompensated in afterlife Having had drunk of the worldly to the bitter dregs, the degenerate Roman aristocracy liked the sensation of the novel practice which would guarantee them a more splendorous life in the Kingdom of Heaven The sensuousness of paganism had been under Christian censure The institution of vestal virgins dedicated to the gods was narrow, because the number of the holy objects of sensuousness was limited. The progeny of Numa had established a monopoly of the privilege The new institution, indeed, flourished under the frowning sign of asceticism, but did not place any limit upon the number of the consecrated virgins. These holy sisters could not always refuse their graces, not of course from themselves, but as the merited gift of God, to the devout Senators who had made such magnificent sacrifice to promote and patronise the angelic institution of monasticism Portly matrons tasted a novel ecstasy by playing devout Magdalenas to the imitations of the Saviour who came to bless them in the tempting persons of sturdy peasant youths from Egypt or Syria Some fair scions of the degenerate aristocracy sought the morbid pleasure of mortifying their flesh, having been sorely disappointed by the limitedness of earthly enjoyment Since there was nothing more to taste of life, they sacrificed but little. In such a state, an illusion is worth immensely more than the enervating feeling of over-satiation Then, should the mortified flesh perchance be refractory and prove too restless for spiritual calm, there were holy brothers at hand to soothe the distressed with a mystical love which would drown the devil of lure in a surging sea of blissful ecstasy.

While the followers of the Egyptian Anthony and Pachonius were conquering pagan Rome, the Syrian desert was populated by the disciples of Hilarion. The Syrian youth passed twelve years of penance, prayer and ascetic life before he became the founder of numerous monasteries in his native land as well as in Palestine. In his travels, the holy man was accompanied by two to three thousand of his most ardent and devoted disciples. Later on, Simeon outshined his predecessor. At the tender age of thirteen, this shepherd youth renounced the world. His ascetic practices are reported to have defied the heat of thirty summers and the cold of as many winters at the top of a column of stone sixty feet high. In addition to the rigour of climate, the holy man, of course, resisted the mighty supernatural forces of evil which came to distract him from the celestial path. He never descended from his lofty position, but went to heaven straight with the glorious crown of voluntary martyrdom. The world that had once marvelled at the sublime speculation of a Plato and was enlightened by the scientific learning of an Aristotle, grovelled at the feet of an illiterate fanatic.

The name and fame of Basil are immortal in monastic history Educated in the schools of Athens, he gave up the Archbishopric of Caesaria and retired into the mountainous fastness of Asia Minor. Later on he founded a chain of monasteries along the coast of the Black Sea

Nor was monasticism confined to the Eastern Provinces of the tottering Roman Empire In the fourth century of the Christian era, the enthusiasm to renounce the world, and practise asceticism, were rampant in Gaul as well as in the distant island of Britain Saint Martin of Tours was a soldier who became a Bishop, and was cannonised for his life of divine purity. Ecclesiastical historians of his time, particularly his biographers, maintain that the desert of the East did not produce any champion of virtue, renunciation and devotion greater than that Gaelic Saint It is reported that two thousand devoted disciples followed the Master to the grave.

More than two thousand devoted ascetics inhabited the famous monastery of Banchor in Flintshire. The monastic movement reached even the obscure corner of Ireland, and the holy home of Saint Colomba was built in a small island of the Hebrides In the fifth century of the Christian era, monks and nuns scattered over the ruins of the Roman Empire— from

Britain to Ethiopia and Spain to the confines of Persia— were counted in millions

These voluntary exiles from social life were impelled by the dark and inexplicable forces of superstition The rapid disintegration of antique society based upon slave labour, and the measures (unbearable taxation etc) adopted to arrest the decline of the Roman Empire, had made worldly life utterly devoid of any hope for the masses Every deluded soul was persuaded that on entering the monastic life, he or she travelled the road to eternal happiness When the worldly life offers absolutely nothing but degenerating poverty, endless misery and a depressing perspective of still deeper degradation, the hope and promise of a mysterious life of eternal happiness can easily become the motive for the renunciation of the sinking ship, and for incredible acts of penance, asceticism and devotion to merit the tempting goal

It is a natural impulse to run away from a house however dear it might have been once, when it cracks and crumbles into a dreary desolation defying all efforts to repair The natural instinct of self-preservation acquires the aura of pious heroism and admirable selflessness only because it is followed with greater enthusiasm, quickened by the alluring vision of a promised land flowing with milk and honey. Simple prudence assumes the complexion of admirable piety Despair appears in the dazzling garb of devotion Natural selfishness undergoes a miraculous metamorphosis, and haughtily misappropriates the doubtful glory of the religious fervour of renunciation Still, to desert a sinking ship with the forlorn hope of reaching the safety of a welcome shore can hardly be distinguished as an act of exceptional bravery, even though it implies the risk of drifting in dark and unknown waters

Under the hopeless conditions of social dissolution, the Christian doctrine of the end of the world was received with frightful credulity. Who would not run away from a world doomed to an early destruction? And since it was encouraged by the temptation of getting a place in the Kingdom of Heaven, the fearful flight naturally became as if it were a stampede of a hungry mob towards an inexhaustible store of food Similarly, when the Hindu persuades himself that the world is but a hallucination, he easily and often cheerfully foregoes its enjoyments, which are placed beyond his reach by the inequities of a religious society. The preconceived notion about the surety of the eternal bliss of a spiritual existence induces the imaginary renunciation of what is not possessed and will never be possessed It is so very much like the disappointed fox who consoled himself with the deception that grapes were sour.

Even such impious and temporal considerations as vanity and worldly power played their part in the spread of monasticism "It was naturally supposed that the pious and humble monks, who had renounced the world to accomplish the work of their salvation, were the best qualified for the spiritual government of the Christians. The reluctant hermit was torn from his cell, and seated, amidst acclamations of the people, on the Episcopal Throne, the monasteries of Egypt, of Gaul and of the East supplied a regular succession of Saints and Bishops, and ambition soon discovered the secret road which led to the possession of wealth and honour .. The popular monks insinuated themselves into noble and opulent homes, and the specious acts of flattery and seduction were employed to secure those proselytes who might bestow wealth or dignity on the monastic profession. . . The credulous maid was betrayed by vanity to violate the laws of nature, and the matron aspired to imaginary perfection by renouncing the virtues of domestic life." (Gibbon)

A critical study of the monastic and akin institutions in India would reveal not a very different picture. Describing the religious Convention of Kanauj, convened by king Harsha-Vardhan (in the first half of the seventh century) and presided over by the famous Chinese monk Huen Tsang, Havell writes "These great church dignitaries from monasteries like that of Nalanda were mounted on elephants, others were carried in palanquins, they were attended by a numerous suit" The Convention over, for twenty days treasures were distributed to the delegates, over ten thousand of whom received hundred pieces of gold each in addition to rich garments, jewels and perfumes In the period of Buddhist ascendency, the Sanghas enjoyed great political power as well as vast material riches. Subsequently, the wealth of the Hindu Maths and Temples became fabulous The monastic orders and priestly hierarchy, while preaching the virtue of renunciation, lived a life of opulence and comfort Imaginary, often fraudulent, spiritual elevation brought material splendour and temporal power to those who might have remained in obscure poverty, had they not resorted to the pretention, imagination and fraud of a holy life Renunciation guaranteed the practitioner of the comfortable cult the means of material subsistence as well as honour, prestige and power Even to-day, the Sadhu enjoys a privileged position in Hindu society. So much so that, while the producing masses are economically bankrupt, the society supports no less than five million religious vagabonds and parasites.

In India, monasticism became rampant during the Buddhist period and continued flourishing after the triumph of Hindu reaction It was in the latter period that the numerous orders of Sadhus and Sanyasis came into existence

The Buddhist monk Upagupta was accompanied by eighteen thousand followers when he met his royal disciple Asoka To celebrate the establishment of Buddhism, Asoka distributed eleven lakh pieces of gold coins to the assembled mendicants The number of religious beggars attending king Harsha's charitable feasts at Prayag, about a thousand years later, was still larger A very substantial percentage of the adult population must have swelled the monastic order during those thousand years It is recorded that the best part of the manhood of the kingdom of Magadha entered the monastic life Buddhist monasticism was analogous to its Christian prototype Both represented despair caused by the collapse of the old social order, and a vain effort to solve the problems of life by running away from it

Asceticism is a perverse ideal,—of a morbid mentality Individual suicide is generally considered to be a reprehensible act. Throughout history, there has been difference of opinion regarding the morality and legality of the act of invidual self-destruction

With all the arguments for and against suicide, it is an incontestable psychological deduction that suicide is committed as a rule in a state of temporary insanity. The virtue of asceticism represents an epidemic of this mental malady. It implies the spread of suicidal mania on a large scale. In other words, the holy man is an assassin. One may be granted the freedom to destroy his tormented self, and his morbid action may be excused as a token of individual insanity But the cult of asceticism, if practised widely, becomes an instrument of homicidal mania Insanity becomes a crime. Individually, the ascetic is to be pitied for his or her depraved insanity, the cult, however, is a veritable crime against humanity The only saving grace is not the silly notion about its spiritualising power, but that it is a social disease as all crimes are When a particular social system is caught in such a severe crisis as overwhelms the multitude with utter despair, suicidal mania finds a fertile field. Insanity becomes epidemic. The world is full of incurable sorrows and sufferings; the only way out is to run away from the world, and seek consolation in the dream of a better existence transcending that of the senses. Parenthood stands in the way of this only escape. Even in the chaos of social decomposition, spiritual egoism cannot always get the better of biological laws expressing themselves as love and affection. Therefore, to secure spiritual uplift, man must sink below the level of animal, must destroy his upsprings even before they are born He must not only make a monstrosity of himself by the futile effort to violate all the laws of nature, he must destroy the posterity, thereby committing gross violence against mother nature herself

Multiplication is the law of nature The social value of asceticism, when it first appeared as a wide-spread cult, was somewhat analogous to that of the modern proletarian movement of birth-control Conscientious people are reluctant to breed progeny when they are not in the position to perform their parental duties But the restraint thus applied to propagation is an obligatory, temporary measure There will be no need for it as soon as the social conditions are changed It does not represent a stupid condemnation of life Besides, the modern movement of birth-control does not propose stifling of the sexual instinct, therefore, the temporary restraint of propagation does not make mental monstrosities out of the living generation But rationalism was unknown to the multitude caught in the crisis of the antique social order The scope and practice of asceticism could not be circumscribed by the consciousness of its social value It was not associated with a conscious revolutionary struggle for overthrowing the decayed social system, which so hopelessly clouded the perspective of life, with the purpose of building up a new society It reflected the despair of the victims of the crisis It was an integral part of the ideology of social dissolution

Not to plunge other souls in the ocean of worldly sorrows, is a motive nobler than spiritual egoism Nevertheless, it also amounts to the same thing, - a reprehensible attempt to destroy the human race. Had religion any place for logic, loyalty or true idealism, then the religious man should revolt against sinful cult which recommends the destruction of the noblest creation of God The teaching of religion is, that God created man after his own image When religion becomes a crime against God himself, there must be something radically wrong with it

The ascetic is a defeatist His defeatism is the product of the depressingly hopeless social conditions that surround him As soon as those conditions change, the disease growing out of them necessarily abates and gradually disappears That was the case with the European society, which succeeded in the struggle to come out of the chaos resulting from the decomposition of the antique society. The virus of Christian monasticism was a passing phenomenon. Manasteries outgrew their original negative features;

gradually, they came to play a positive social role as productive units which constituted the corner - stone of a new social order In India, the social crisis became a chronic disease, the ugly symptoms of which perpetuated themselves as so many specific features of a special type of culture Raising defeatism on the proud pedestal of imaginary and often fraudulent spirituality, Indian society abjured the path of struggle It stagnated into a fossilised existence, the " conservative genius " of which choked the internal forces of disruption and progress, but could not resist violent impacts from outside The Hindu ideal of Brahmcharya is a hideous heritage of a tragic past

In the world of early Christianity as well as in India, monasteries were filled mostly by the destitute who gained much more in the new life of renunciation than they had actually sacrificed. It has been ascertained by critical historians that the great majority of the inmates of the Christian monasteries were pauperised peasants, run - away slaves and destitute artisans For those unfortunate victims of a social catastrophy the new life was a welcome escape from hopeless poverty, unbearable extortions and endless hardships They left a perilous life of dishonour and contempt for a safe and laudable profession The destitute and down-trodden scum of the earth became the chosen elite whose entrance into the glorious Kingdom of Heaven was assured The austerities of monastic life were a very inconsiderable price to be paid for the invaluable reward The physical hardships and privations of the holy profession were easily borne by the brothers and sisters accustomed to manual labour in the world They were borne cheerfully, since those enlisted in the service of the God were guaranteed the indispensable necessities of life, which had not been always and easily available to them before The ecclesiastical historian Tilemont writes that in Egypt, for example, " a monk lived more comfortably than a shepherd " No wonder that destitute shepherds enthusiastically embraced monastic life, which transformed them into proud and privileged leaders of the swarms of devout bipeds, instead of the scarce and costly sheep they no longer possessed to tend

For more than two hundred years, all the inmates of the Buddhist monasteries were also recruited from the poor oppressed classes Havell writes : "For over two centuries, the Buddhist Sanghas were not influential enough to win many powerful patrons among the Aryan aristocracy, either Brahman or Kshatriya. It became the State religion only after it had outgrown its original revolutionary fervour Then the doors of the opulent monasteries were closed to the down - trodden It was ordained by the temporal laws that the Sanghas should not be used as a means of escaping secular obligations or evading the laws of the State No one could enter them to avoid payment of debts, criminals under punishment, deserters from royal services and slaves were also excluded" Evidently, until then the Sanghas had offered a hospitable refuge to those unfortunate social outcastes.

The social background of the Christian cult of monasticism has been depicted by Gibbon as follows · "The subjects of Rome, whose persons and fortunes were made responsible for unequal and exorbitant tributes, retired from the oppression of the imperial government, and pusillanimous youths preferred the penance of a monastic, to the dangers of a military life The afrighted provincials of every rank, who fled before the barbarians, found shelter and subsistence (in monasteries), whole legions were buried in these religious sanctuaries and the same cause which relieved the distress of individuals impaired the strength of the empire" In many a classical treatise on the Roman law, particularly the Justinian Code, we read of measures to enforce the private and public obligations of citizenship; but the laws of a decrepit government were too feeble a dam to resist the fierce current of superstition so bountifully fed with the consternation caused by an insurmountable social chaos.

Exactly similar causes were in operation also in India. As an admirer of the spiritual essence of Indo - Aryan culture, Havell can be trusted to make a proper appreciation of monasticism Nevertheless, he writes . "Monastic life was held in so high esteem and offered so many attractions to the Kshatriya youths, that the fighting strength of Aryawarta was becoming dangerously weakened, and the resources of the State needed for national defence were absorbed by the thousands of monasteries filled with the wearers of the yellow robe" Again, " The conquest of Sindh by the Arabs was made easy by the fact that thousands of the male population had adopted the yellow robe for the sake of the easy life of the monastery The monastic system continued to absorb a large proportion of the flower of Indian manhood even after the development of Brahman philosophy."

All the persecutions and repressions of the Hindu kings proved impotent to stem the tide of Buddhist Nihilism. Pushyamitra, who overthrew the Buddhist Maurya dynasty and assumed the leadership of Brahmanical reaction, deprived the monastic order of all power in the State, acquired since the time of

Asoka Monasteries were forcibly dissolved, and monks persecuted everywhere. Yet, monasticism could not be stamped out It kept on flourishing in the face of persecution. Monasticism had become such a serious social menace that, after the death of Asoka, the Maurya rulers tried to check its ruinous progress by imposing heavy penalties upon those who left their families without provision But the flood tide of social dissolution could not be resisted. It swept away the splendid empire of the Mauryas.

The sagacity of the Indian Constantine, Asoka, sought, and to some extent succeeded, to furnish the ideology of social dissolution for the defence and even consolidation of the decayed social order by pandering demonstratively to the vanity of monasticism Under the royal patronage of Asoka and his successors, Buddhism stopped short of running its cataclysmic course of Nihilism; and that very deviation from its basic principle ultimately caused the downfall of Buddhism and the re-establishment of Brahman orthodoxy In order to be victorious, Christianity also capitulated to the obstinate forces of pagan superstition, but the hybrid religion of the Catholic Church retained the original name of Christianity. In the case of Buddhism, the capitulation was complete. Even the name had to go, in return for a place conceded to its founder in the list of the legendary Avatars of Hinduism. The superstitious practices of Hinduism corrupted and caused the downfall of Buddhism But the vanquished was avenged by the fact that its most characteristic feature - monasticism - passed on to the triumphant religion The hero of the conquering host, Sankaracharya himself, was the founder of the most powerful and abiding monastic order.

Critical investigation will bring into light the fact that behind the apparent prosperity of the Buddhist era, there operated similar social forces as promoted the abnormal phenomenon of monasticism in the period of decay and decline of the Roman Empire Meanwhile, recorded history as well as social science warrant the assertion that the great majority of the Buddhist monks, and later on Hindu Sadhus and Sanyasis, must have been recruited from the masses of peasants and artisans rendered destitute and desperate by all the factors indicating a severe social crisis, namely, decay of the roots of the established economic system, the resulting decline of industry and trade, pauperisation of the masses, increasing burden of taxation and various other forms of extortions, and political oppression Before the establishment of Buddhism as the State religion, propagandists of the new faith - Bhikkhus - travelled from village to village, preaching to the poor, destitute and the outcastes. Old records show that the majority of the monks and nuns were recruited from the villages, that is, from the economically ruined and socially oppressed masses

Uncritical historians, particularly those with nationalist predilections, confound the greatness with the happiness of a nation The greatness of a nation in the past is erroneously measured by the magnificence of the royal court and the opulence of the ruling aristocracy It is conveniently overlooked who paid for that greatness and splendour, and what was the condition of the multitude who tilled and toiled so that the rulers could put on the flattering garb of greatness, magnificence, and renown Invariably, the life of the multitude was devoted, not voluntarily but under duress, to produce the material that went into the making of that glorious garb of equivocal greatness.

In the early and mediaeval ages, the productivity of labour was necessarily much lower than at present. Consequently, exceptional grandeur of royal cities, imposing magnificence of courts, flaunting extravagance of the nobility, vain stateliness of public and private architecture and the wasteful richness of temples and mausoleums, were not possible unless national income was very disproportionately distributed. As a matter of fact, those very monuments of national greatness testify to the endless oppression and grinding poverty of the masses They represented a futile effort to conceal the decay of the established social order and the consequent destitution and degradation of the people. Historical research has revealed the fact that external splendour of the Roman Empire reached the apex just when the barbarous system of slavery was eating into the very foundations of the imperial structure. That was the era of Augustus and Constantine. Later on, Justinian satisfied his vanity of eclipsing the magnificence of his vain - glorious predecessors just when the economic fabrics of the empire were in ruins, and wide - spread bankruptcy and destitution of the toiling masses were flaming the superstition of monasticism.

For the construction of the Great Wall of China, more than twenty - five per cent of the entire social labour was withdrawn from productive activities. The result inevitably was a disastrous famine which reduced the population of the country by half. It was precisely in that period that Buddhist monasticism flourished in China, and the impatience for the bliss of Nirwana urged thousands of unhappy fanatics to the incredible practice of hurling themselves down from high mountains which, by virtue of those inhuman acts, acquired the reputation of possessing miraculous charms.

There is absolutely no reason to believe that the national grandeur of India from the time of Asoka to the reign of Harsavardhan and right up to the invasion of Mahmud of Ghazni was reared upon a different social basis Had it been so, the same period of greatness would not find such a considerable part of the population abandoning the natural life of a social being to adopt the morbid monastic profession Had the people enjoyed worldly happiness when their rulers were basking in the sun of grandeur and glory, they would not rush madly after an illusion, leaving the reality behind Havell writes "Every great temple which was built, meant the dedication of public and private funds for the maintenance of priests, temple servants, Brahman student and their gurus, Sadhus and Sanyasis And it was the period from the seventh century to the time of Mahmud of Ghazni, which was the most prolific in religious building, - a time when Hindu monarchs vied with each other in the magnificence and number of their temples, when sacred hills were converted into cities of the gods, and when hundreds and thousands of skilled artisans were diverted from ordinary industrial pursuits to the pious labour of elaborating the embellishment of the temple service in stone, bronze, precious metal and costly fabrics" ('The Aryan Rule of India').

It was not an easy task to preserve the holy appearance of an abnormal institution embracing an ever-increasing multitude of social derelicts, actuated by motives far from being genuinely spiritual. It was however, accomplished through the destruction of the freedom of mind by fomenting the virtue of credulity and encouraging the merit of submission. The mind of a superstitious crowd steeped in ignorance and trembling with fear, submitted to the most absurd and atrocious habits, the fanatical practice of which would be rewarded surely with salvation, and possibly even with worldly fame, power and prestige Austerities, that have been claimed as the special merit of the holy men of India, were carried to incredible extent by Christian monks. Pleasure and guilt were synonymous terms in the monastic vocabulary of India as well as of any other country inflicted by the disease. Everywhere impure desires of the flesh were mortified by the rigour of fast and abstemiousness Church Fathers like Saint Jerome were enthusiastically eloquent about the spiritual effect of fasting and abstinence. The inmates of Eastern monasteries-disciples of Anthony and Pachonius - lived on the pittance of twelve ounces of dry bread a day, and had to perform hard labour to keep their minds away from evil thoughts Nights were devoted to prayer, penance and meditation. Meat eating was strictly forbidden, and water was the only beverage compatible with the spiritual life of a man The early Christian ideal of evangelical poverty was the last word of the doctrine of renunciation On entering the holy life, the monk abjured all earthly possessions, the cloak on his back was not to be called his own The holy man lived on alms or the product of manual labour performed in the service of God.

Such a comfortless and barren life was naturally tormented by evil spirits, which are nothing but the vision of vainly suppressed desires and haunted by hallucinations The life of every Christian Saint is a tale of heroic struggle against the temptations of Satan and of miraculous victories over those sources of evil. Since every prisoner of monasticism was either a miniature or an incipient saint, he also must experience the struggles and triumphs of the thorny road to holiness How familiar are we in India with the tales of such spiritual exploits ! But here as well as in many other countries, these tales were so hungrily devoured by the credulous multitude, because the hopeless conditions of their miserable life could be possibly changed only by a miracle. Recording some of those legends about the Christian Saints, and exposing their spurious origin, Gibbon writes "These extravagant tales, which display the fiction, without genius, of poetry, have seriously affected the reason, the faith, and the morals of the Christians. Their credulity debased and vitiated the faculties of the mind; they corrupted the evidence of history; and superstition gradually extinguished the hostile light of philosophy and science Every mode of religious worship which had been practised by the Saints, every mysterious doctrine which they had believed, was fortified by the sanction of divine revelation, and all the manly virtues were oppressed by the servile and pusillanimous reign of the monks."

One composing a critical history of ancient India could use this admirable passage verbatim for summarising our spiritual heritage, which has been such a stout bulwark of reaction for centuries, and has contributed so much to our present unenviable plight The European nations recovered from the virulent plague germinated in the putrid carcass of the once magnificent Roman Empire, as soon as the advance of knowledge raised the depressing gloom hanging upon life. The happy dawn of knowledge was caused by the rise of forces building a new social order Only the faith in the endless possibilities of worldly life can persuade man to abandon the vain chase after the will-o-the-wisp of an imaginary sublimer existence which disregards all reality This wild race after a chimera ceases only when man regains faith in himself, and by the strength of advancing knowledge throws off the influence of credulity, prejudice and superstition.

The supine complacence and idle pride regarding the sublimity of our spiritual heritage should no longer lull the critical faculty of the progressive Indians. Legendary glorification of a past sickness should not curb the striving for a fuller life of health and real happiness But, for the purpose deceptive bubbles must be burst, legends deprived of the fraudulent garb of history, and credulity confronted with criticism Unless we know how to read correctly the history of our past, we shall never be able to survive our present degradation, and conquer a future of real greatness.

IRRELIGIOSITY AND ATHEISM OF HINDU PHILOSOPHY

The doctrine of creation out of nothing is an essential element of religious thought. The Bible sets forth this cardinal dogma in the most logical as well as orthodox form The fullest play is given to the concept of Omnipotence There is no attempt to tamper or temper it with reason The very notion being absurd, its absurdity must be manifest in its practical expression, unless its pristine purity is adulterated, and, in that case, the faithful would be so much less religious because of the imperfectness of their faith in the basic dogma of religion. The doctrine of creation out of nothing is the counter-part of the conception of a personal God. This idea is the very essence of religion and Monotheism is the highest form of religion

Miracle - mongering is another feature of Christianity, which is usually laughed at by the advocates of "scientific" religion. Hinduism is dogmatically claimed to be the only religion possessing that destructive distinction. If the claim had any foundation of reality, then the distinction would mean the extinction of Hinduism as a religion. As a matter of fact, the positive significance of ancient Hindu philosophy was to liquidate Hinduism as a religion.

Science and faith are mutually exclusive, and there can be no religion without faith. The fantastic idea of a "scientific" religion is expounded by irreligious spiritualists - that queer breed of modern intellectuals, who pompously deride scientific knowledge, while possessing no faith, who grope blindly in the twilight of the borderland of darkness and light. Miracle-mongering is the practical expression of the faith in God, that is, in God as God the Almighty. Since the world is the creation of an almighty power, not bound by the laws of nature - of space, time and causality - anything can happen any time and anywhere. This belief is the very breath of religion. Untrammelled by the zeal for rewriting history to fit into a scheme laid a priori, anybody could see that every Hindu even to-day believes in miracle. Otherwise, the face of Mother India would have changed unrecognisably long ago.

The stories of the Ramayana and Mahabharata are full of miracles The epic heroes are miracles personified The Hindu masses implictly believe in those stories, it is sinful to doubt their veracity The modern intellectual confidently talks of the ancient glory of India on the strength of "the historical facts" contained in the epics. The miraculous acts and movements of the epic heroes are considered to offer indisputable evidence in support of the utterly unhistorical contention that several thousand years ago, India attained a level of scientific and technological development not yet surpassed by the modern civilisation This contention beats the most fundamentalist Christian, in the faith in miracle In the utter absence of social conditions, requisite for any advance in that direction, the supposed, rather imagined, scientific and technological attainments could be possible only as a miracle

The faith in the supernatural powers of the Yogi is also a faith in miracle There are few even among the modern educated Indians who would not look upon the usual feats of any ordinary magician (sleight of hand or charlatanry) as evidence invalidating scientific theories; who would not find the hand of God in any natural phenomenon that cannot as yet be scientifically explained As regards the masses of the

Hindu population, even to-day the faith in miracle is as living as it was with the Christians in the early middle-ages. For example, faced with illness, individual or epidemic, the vast bulk of the rural population would much rather seek relief in some sort of religious ceremony than rely upon the curative value of medical and hygienic agencies The supernatural power of Sadhus and Sanyasis is a matter of general belief Otherwise, how could several millions of these parasites still thrive upon the poverty of the masses? The spell and influence of these religious parasites are not based upon any other spiritual merit than the superstitious belief in their supernatural power. Mahatma Gandhi's great popularity among the masses is only to a very small extent due to the awakening political consciousness. It is mostly due to a wide-spread belief in his power to do what ordinary mortals cannot, - that is, in his power to do miracles. That is why he has been cannonised as a Mahatma.

The belief in miracle is the result of a lack of self-confidence Had the modern Indians been less addicted to the faith in miracle than the early and mediaeval Christians, they would have shown greater ability to change the dismal conditions of their country The fact that the bulk of those engaged in the struggle for temporal power have been worshipping for years at the shrine of a Mahatma, proves that they expect to be saved by a miracle.

If one did not stand firmly and unconditionally by the belief that God created the world somehow, by virtue of his Omnipotence, out of nothing, without any material substance, if one did not implicitly believe, as the corollary to this faith in the Almightiness of God, in all sorts of magic and miracles, then there would arise inevitably the fatal question How did God create the world? - a question that at once transcends the boundary of religion, and leads, sooner or later, directly or indirectly, to naturalism, atheism, materialism, that is, to real philosophy.

Provoked by the doubt inherent in the mystical speculations of the Upanishads, the earlier systems of Hindu philosophy - Vaisheshik and Sankhya - tried to answer the dangerous question without having raised it explicitly. The essence of those two earlier systems of philosophy eventually contributed to the rise of Buddhist atheism. All the heavy artillery of Vedic fundamentalism had to be put in action for combatting, and ultimately destroying, that disruptive doctrine. But Sankaracharya himself realised that his speculative and arbitrary interpretation of the Vedanta Sutras, done with the purpose of combatting Buddhism and the semi-materialist systems of philosophy that had gone into its making, could not serve its purpose except by contradicting itself through the postulation of a personal God Otherwise, even the hallucination of the world could not be "explained" within the limits of religious thought His pantheistic interpretation of Vedanta, if carried to its logical conclusion, itself leads to Materialism That line of logical development was avoided by the arbitrary relapse to the anthropomorphic conception of God, the retreat was covered by a mass of sophistry and hopeless confusion, - all serving the one purpose of self-deception. Christianity also headed towards the slippery path of idealist philosophy as soon as it left the strictly religious ground, to wander into the labyrinth of theology But in the beginning, it was a pure form of spiritualism, because of its uncompromising conception of a personal God, and firm attachment to the virgin faith associated with such a pure religious conception.

Denial of the objective reality of the material world is the foundation of spiritualism It is divested of its purely dogmatic character only when it is inferred from the doctrine of creation out of nothing, which, in its turn, must be inseparably associated with the idea of a personal God. That which is once created is bound to disappear It does not really exist. It is a phantom. Transitoriness is identical with unreality.

Those are the cardinal principles of religious philosophy The validity of those arguments depends on the belief in a personal God.

The personal God is the real God, because all the supernatural and unnatural attributes ascribed to the Supreme Being by spiritualism can be logically associated only with the anthropomorphic concept. The Supreme Being is supposed to be beyond all limitations. In order to fit into the rôle allotted to him by his creators (God is the creation of the religious man), the Supreme Being must be unconditionally free The belief in the possibility of the creation of the physical universe out of no available material represents the highest concept of freedom, and Omnipotence is born of unlimited freedom. The two conceptions can never be separated without losing force; and they can assume the appearance of reality only in a personal God.

Supernatural powers and attributes must remain empty conceptions, unrealities, so long as they are not conceived as the powers and attributes of a Subject. That is to say, spiritual (supernatural) categories become conceivable only when they are associated with the idea of a personal God. One possessed of the unbounded freedom of creating endless things out of no given substance, is really above, beyond, and uncircumvented by the material being. He is the real spiritual existence par excellence Creation out of nothing is an act by which the creator is not bound, because there is no causal connection between the two. The personal God does not create out of necessity. He does it out of sheer whim or arbitrariness, - the corollary to his Omnipotence. The freedom of his will is altogether unbounded. Since he creates, not out of necessity, but of sweet will, he may or may not create He is not bound to create Thus he is absolutely free of any material existence. He is an absolutely pure spiritual being The personal God of strictly monotheistic religions, such as Christianity and Islam, therefore, is not a sign of childish credulity, spiritual inferiority, on the contrary, the concept represents the highest pitch of religious, that is, spiritualist thought The absurdity is not hidden behind subtile doctrines, nor made to appear plausible in a mirage of mysticism, it is boldly and faithfully carried to its logical climax

A religion should be measured by religious standards Spiritualism must be judged by the purity of its spirituality. A body of religious thought that can attain the point of culmination indicated by itself, without ceasing to be strictly religious, that is, without deviating from the straight path of faith, is spiritualism of the purest water. So long as religion can stand frankly as itself, on its own merit, without being ashamed of its absurdity, without feeling any necessity of hiding its naked beauty of barbarism in ill - fitting draperies of deception, so long it should be considered as performing a useful social function. After that, it can stand only as an artificial structure obstructing further spiritual progress.

As against the purely spiritualist idea of personal God of the strictly monotheistic religions, the Supreme Being of Hindu Pantheism (particularly of the Vedanta) is not a free agent If it is really Nirakara and Nirvikara, it cannot be the cause of the world. But only in the state of absolute rest it is so. Presently that absolute spiritual state is disturbed, and the Supreme Being manifests itself as the world of phenomena The seed sprouts and becomes the tree. The spirit becomes matter The spiritual Supreme Being is bound to the material existence by causal connection Two things cannot stand in the relation of causality — one the cause, the other effect — unless there is something common in them The pantheist Spinoza, compelled by the rigorous logic of the mathematical precision of his philosophy, came to this conclusion, and consequently showed that consistent pantheism holds in itself the germ of materialism

The Supreme Being of pantheism is not purely spiritual, because it is identical with the material world, the latter being dormant in the former, when not manifested. It is generally admitted that an act must be preceded by a desire. The doctrine of creation ascribes desire to God, and thereby limits his absoluteness and brings him down to the human level. But the anxiety of theology and religious philosophy to divest God of his humanness, destroys him as a religious reality. God can have the force of a real existence for the religious, only as a highly idealised man, a superman, free from the limitations of man, yet after all built after human model. The anxiety to rationalise the concept of God - to divest him of the human propensity to createdeprives God of his genuine godliness, of his ability to be really unbounded by matter, robs him of his reality, of his raison d'être.

"Religion is the dream of humanity. But even in dream, we are not wafted in the realm of Nothingness or in Heaven. We still remain in the realm of reality—on the earth, only we do not see real things in the light of reality and necessity, but in the dazzling shimmer of imagination and arbitrariness. "(Ludwig Feuerbach, "The Essence of Christianity").

To deprive God of his religious reality is to abolish him. To rationalise God into a metaphysical and mystical Supreme Being, whose being, by its very nature, does not possess the force of religious reality, is to deny the existence of God The conception of God is an irrational conception Religion cannot be reconciled with reason The honestly religious, that is, the consistent spiritualist, must not be ashamed of his enumeration with the old dame Faith, and check the inclination to flirt with the fashionable Reason. Any attempt to rationalise religion, to shift its basis from faith to reason, is bound to be caught in a vicious circle of irreconcilable contradictions The religious conception of God, as a supernatural being, contradicts reason On the other hand, a God, conceived logically as the universal spirit, a synthetic God so to say, is no God For by its very nature, such a God is the creation of human reason.

The Hindu pantheist doctrine of emanation or evolution, which claims spiritual superiority over the strictly religious doctrine of creation, either identifies the Supreme Being with its absolute attributes, or denudes it of all attributes In any case, it divests God of Omnipotence and unbounded freedom, because the doctrine of emanation robs God of the prerogative to create at his will. This doctrine does not allow God the freedom of creating or not creating, as he pleases. At the ruinous cost of his absolute power and unbounded freedom, God is cleansed of the human blemish of desire - to create But the doctrine that places him in this position of doubtful advantage, hopelessly compromises his pure spirituality According to this damaging doctrine, creation does not take place in consequence of a desire on the part of God. It makes emanation (another name for creation) of the phenomenal world a process inherent in the Supreme Being The Supreme Being is thus eternally and inseparably associated with matter. Indeed, matter is inherent in its very being The insistence on the pure spirituality of the Supreme Being compels the admission that, parallel to it, there exists eternally a non-spiritual substance, in germinal condition, at any rate If the Supreme Being is granted any directive, controlling or initiative function in connection with the evolution and involution of the material substance, then the doctrine of creation comes back surreptitiously. The difference is that the stature of God is reduced at least by half, for he may still have the freedom to create or not to create, but he can create only with the material which exists independent of, at any rate parallel to, himself. Moreover, actually he does not possess the freedom He is bound to create; otherwise, the process inherent in the eternally existing material substance would go on, and the function of the Supreme Being become obsolete.

To evade this catastrophe, pantheism does not admit the parallel existence of matter. It is identified with the spirit. But the pantheist doctrine of emanation destroys the spiritualism of the unitary primal existence. Since the material world grow out of it, it must contain matter in embryo. So, either the problem of dualism comes back to make of God an useless fixture, or the unity can be preserved only as a material unity Even the most fantastic extravagance of pantheism — Mayavad — does not guarantee the pure spirituality of the Supreme Being. The doctrine of emanation implies determinism. To unfold itself in the form of the world of phenomena, be it real or a hallucination, is inherent in the Supreme Being. That is to say, its movements are determined by its own laws. Freedom disappears. An existence, subjected to determinism, is conditioned; therefore, it cannot be spiritual.

Then, there still remains the most elementary difficulty. Existence means extension in space. That which is limited by the material concept of space, cannot be spiritual, which, to be itself, must transcend the limitation of space as well as of time and causality. In the attempt - of theology and religious philosophy- to free religion of its native irrationality, to camouflage the primitive doctrine of creation out of nothing, God is shorn of his unbounded freedom, of his arbitrary will completely unrestricted by anything else existing outside of himself, and is placed in the disgraceful position of subordination, if not directly of matter, but in any case of the law of determinism which obliges him to bring forth the physical phenomena of the universe, which again, obeying the imperious law of determinism, go their own way disregarding the will of the Supreme Being

Pantheist mysticism not only deprives God of his religious reality, it undermines teleology which is the corner-stone of spiritualist philosophy It pretends to obviate the baffling question How could the material come out of the spiritual, the impure out of the pure, the dark out of the light ? The magical feat is performed by the simple device of placing nature in God The origin of matter is discovered in the spirit, of darkness in light, of the ungodly in the God Since matter cannot originate in spirit without the latter losing its spirituality, darkness cannot emerge from light, the ungodly cannot be inherent in the godly being, the magical feat of pantheist mysticism is simply to declare matter, darkness and ungodliness to be as eternal as the spiritual existence. The old problem of philosophy - the problem of dualism is not solved It is simply mystified, transplanted in the very being of God The fundamental doctrine of religion is sacrilegiously sacrificed by a pseudo-philosophy, which seeks to rationalise religion.

To blow up God into nothingness is atheism, even if this iconoclastic process takes place as a higher form of spiritualism To debase spirit to the level of matter by subordinating it to determinism, is the height of irreligiosity, is the negation of spiritualism, although this devastating process of self-consummation takes place as an attack upon materialism. But the development is a necessary process Every form of thought contains in itself the germ of its liquidation in favour of a higher form of thought Religion necessarily leads to theology - the futile speculative attempt to define the nature of God Theology is futile speculation, because it can never perform the task it sets to itself As soon as human mind can define him, God cease to be God Therefore, the historical function of theology is to destroy religion, as religion. Having destroyed its own source, theology destroys itself. Consistently developed, theology culminates into pantheism. In the pantheistic form, theology consumes itself. Consistent pantheism leads to atheism Thus goes on the dialectic process of ideological development It is not possible to declare any one point in this process as its climax, and stop there

Christian spiritualism, having reached the pantheistic stage, consumed itself - in the philosophy of Spinoza and Hegel That, in its turn, found the logical development in modern materialism A similar liquidation of the Vedantic pantheism would be the positive outcome of Hindu philosophy. But owing to historical reasons, Indian thought failed to advance beyond the pantheistic stage The development of Hindu pantheism towards its logical conclusion was arrested during the long period of social stagnation that followed the unfortunate defeat of the Buddhist revolution. One misfortune bred another in succession and Indian thought remained stationary. The world went ahead. The logic of historical development is that, as soon as the prolonged social stagnation will be broken, Indian thought also will go rapidly ahead from the point at which it temporarily stopped, and catch up with the progress made by others.

European thought also remained entangled in mystic-pantheist spiritualism for more than a thousand years after the revolutionary role of early Christianity had been played out. Finally it came out of the vicious circle. It has been India's fate to linger longer in the darkness of decayed spiritualism. She also must come out of that darkness, if she desires to join the progressive march of humanity. The world does not need her message of mystic-pantheist spiritualism The Western civilisation has had the experience of that bliss, and has finally produced something superior India herself should be able to learn the true message of her ancient philosophy. The correct evaluation of that philosophy will be to discern the germ of materialism imbedded in it In order to draw practical inspiration from the heritage of the past, the leaders of modern India must learn to appreciate the positive outcome of Indian philosophy, which amounts to the liquidation of the religious mode of thought. The highest appreciation of the ancient Hindu philosophy will be to find out how it can helps us out of the vicious circle of decayed spiritualism, and indicate the way to real spiritual freedom offered by the materialist philosophy

WHAT IS MARXISM ?

Lately, Marxism has become quite familiar in our country, particularly among the young intellectuals. But I must tell you in the beginning that, as far as I could gather, it is rather the terms that is familiar than what the term stands for Therefore, the question is quite pertinent, and it is quite proper that the subject of this essay has been formulated in the interrogative By Marxism is generally understood some form of politics or some economic doctrines. Certainly economics and politics come under the general term of Marxism. But economics and politics are but parts, and rather subsidiary parts, of what Marxism essentially is. Marxism, essentially, is a philosophy. But it is distinguished from other philosophies inasmuch as it is not a closed system of philosophy.

Marxism is a philosophy, but it is not a system of doctrines, it is not a bunch of dogmas. It is rather a method Those who claim to give a wider interpretation of Marxism, define it as economic interpretation of history That also is a vulgar interpretation of Marxism For one thing Marxian interpretation of history is not economic, but Marxism gives a materialistic interpretation of history, and Materialism is not concerned with bread and butter Marxism includes economic theories, political doctrines and a program of political action Because Marxism is a philosophy of life As a philosophy of life, it must include every department of human activity, and economics and politics are matters which concern human life It is necessary to raise the question What is Marxism, and to answer it because, if we want to apply Marxian theories in life, in the economic and political spheres of our life, it is necessary to understand the essentials of Marxism. If we do not do that, we transform Marxism into a bunch of dogmas and, instead of revolutionaries, we become mystics

The philosophy which is called Marxism is a materialistic philosophy In other words, Marxism is materialistic philosophy But Marxian Materialism is very different from what is usually known as Materialism

To begin with, we must know one thing, namely, that what is called Marxism is not revealed wisdom What is known as the teachings of Karl Marx are not products of the mind of one individual The historical significance and value of the teachings of Karl Marx is to be found in the fact that they are a co-ordination, a systematisation and a clear scientific presentation of the entire product of human thought, and human activity during the three or four hundred years which preceded the time of Karl Marx (You all know that during the 15th and 16th century, European humanity went through a profound revolution That was a philosophical and cultural revolution which preceded the great political and social revolutions of the eighteenth century The positive outcome of that revolution was a revolution of human values Until then, human thought had been flowing in one channel. It had exhausted all its possibilities. It had ended in the blind alley of mysticism and the teleological view of life For the further progress of humanity, it was necessary to free human spirit from the bondage of religion, from the bondage of faith That was made possible by the discoveries of Copernicus and Galileo and other great pioneers of modern science.)

In order to understand Marxism properly, it will be necessary for you to begin with a definition of philosophy We say Marxism is a philosophy. Therefore, we must begin with defining philosophy itself. What is philosophy ? There is a great deal of confusion on this question, and I do not think that two philosophers can be found who agree on their own subject. But if we study the history of philosophy, we shall be compelled to come to the conclusion that philosophy is nothing but the explanation of the Universe in terms of tangible quantities If you go back to the origin of philosophy, in the East as well as in the West, you will find that its foundation is rationalism It begins with the effort to explain human existence and the environments of human existence That primitive effort to explain the world was bound to end in failure, because without scientific knowledge regarding the structure of the physical Universe and the operation of the forces involved in the physical Universe it is impossible to give a comprehensive explanation in physical terms

Now, it is generally believed that religion is inherent in man It is said that to believe is human nature. There again, close acquaintance with the history of humanity leads us to believe the contrary. It is not human nature to believe. Human nature is to enquire The essence of human nature is to find the causes of things Man, by nature, is rationalist, and philosophy was born by the questionings of the primitive man Faith stepped in only when the primitive man failed in his effort to give an explanation of the Universe in terms of tangible quantities, in physical terms But we cannot leave a thing without explanation When we cannot explain a thing, not knowing its cause, we must assume suppositions / The philosophy known as Marxism is the logical outcome, of the scientific mode of thought.) The essence of thought is not to accept anything for granted If your enquiry requires hypothesis, it should not be granted any more value than of hypothesis For a scientist, a hypothesis has to be established through empirical investigation The scientific thought introduced in our modern time by the founders of classical modern philosophy, dissolved the religious mode of thought which had dominated European thought during the preceding 1000 or 1200 years But rationalist philosophy, which could give a complete explanation of the Universe is naturally dependent on the advance of science Consequently, the efforts of the founders of modern philosophy to construct a closed system of thought compelled them to fall back on metaphysical assumptions, where science did not supply them with the clue for the solution of a problem. Modern philosophy was caught in that vicious circle until Karl Marx. The vicious circle was that it started with the repudiation of all previous metaphysical assumptions, but had to set up new metaphysical assumptions I can only remind you of Kant His philosophy has gone down in history as the all-shattering philosophy He destroyed all the old, and built up a new system of metaphysics This was not entirely due to the backwardness of natural sciences There was another reason, namely certain errors in epistemology, in the theory of cognition In their anxiety to dispense with everything that could appear as immaterial, the founders of modern Materialism underestimated the rôle of the mind There were fantastic doctrines which regarded mind as a secretion of the brain, or similar doctrines If you go to that extent, then you are confronted with the fundamental problem in epistemology, namely how is knowledge possible ? This question baffled all, and in the absence of a scientific explanation, these fantastic doctrines were set up Marx could brush away the cobwebs of this old philosophy only by giving an answer to this baffling question On that point, the fundamental principle of Marx is that ideas are also realities You know the old controversy regarding the ultimate reality of either idea or matter, spirit or matter. Now, the earlier materialists disputed the reality of ideas, of the mind By reality is understood objective reality. Marx was the first materialist to recognise the objective reality of ideas He said that once ideas are formed, once the process of ideation has taken place in human mind, ideas are as real as any other physical object. That gives a new complexion to the whole controversy. Ideas are matter, ideas and their object are no longer antithetical terms, but it becomes a question of priority. Which precedes what ? Did idea precede the physical world ? Or did matter precede idea ? Marx did not try to give a speculative answer to that question He went in for an exhaustive examination of the development of human ideas In that attempt he was not the pioneer (The pioneer work was done by Hegel, the ideological preceptor of Karl Marx Hegel, for the first time, had written a coherent history of philosophy and come to the conclusion that the history of mankind is the history of philosophy He said that ideas existed and the material world is the relation of ideas.) Now Marx raised the question How do ideas come into existence ? In the olden days, when human mind was accustomed to religious thought, this question could appear as irrelevant. But in the age of scientific thought, it is perfectly relevant and had to be answered If it is true that the history of mankind is the history of philosophy, the clue to the history of mankind that is the governing law of social evolution, will be found in the origin of idea Once an idea is formed, human behaviour and development is dominated by this idea. But how are these ideas formed ? Once we can find that, we will be able to find the fundamental law of social development.

By investigating the origin of society, and aided by the material collected by other sciences, for example anthropology, archeology and others, (Marx could establish that the mode of thinking of human beings is determined by the mode by which he earns his livelihood.) That reduces all problems to a very simple substratum. Marxian philosophy may not be entirely accepted by all the philosophers to-day But no philosopher who is worthy of the name, much less any scientist, would dispute that our mode of thought, our behaviours, our beliefs, are determined by the environments in which we live This is no longer a matter of theory or speculation, but a matter of fact, and these are not mere historical facts, which we have to discover by research in antiquity But we find them before our own eyes if we study the mode of living of people in other parts of the world (We can see that different groups of people, living in different parts of the world, invariably develop different modes of production, have distinct ideas, distinct kinds of faiths and distinct social organisations.) When Marx could make that discovery, the old problem of philosophy, that is the epistemological problem, how knowledge is possible, was solved. For the first time, we had an insight into history We had a certain fundamental principle which could explain the entire human existence in its various departments Therefore, Marxism is not limited only to philosophy, but it stretches out to all the other branches of human activity But you must remember that there is Marxism, and again we say this is Marxist economics, or Marxist politics That means, we approach these latter problems of economics and politics in the light of certain principles which are the principles of Marxian philosophy We approach all the problems in this same light The essence of Marxism is in those principles, which are the principles of Materialism

Having come to that conclusion, Marx gave a new definition of philosophy itself He said that the task of philosophy is not to interpret the world, but to remake the world Until the time of Marx, philosophy was nothing but speculation It tried to interpret the world It accepted the world as it is, and tried to explain it But it did not raise the question, why things exist as they do, or how this existence came about It simply regarded the physical universe as something existing, with certain practices going on, and tried to explain how they were going on. But why it was so, philosophy did not attempt to find out, and somehow or other it invariably ended in metaphysical assumptions Explanation was given by resorting to some Universal Will, some Higher Purpose, or as modern metaphysics puts it (nothing but realisation of ideas ?

According to the old conception, the philosopher had nothing to do with life itself He can only contemplate the panorama of the physical universe. Everyone started from a certain premise and one had no right to challenge the premise Once one accepted it, one had also to accept a rounded system of philosophy that followed from that premise But now for the first time the premise itself was challenged by the philosophy which is called Marxism According to Marxian philosophy, man can give an explanation of the Universe, because man has a hand in the creation of the Universe

The object of philosophy is not to interpret the world, but to re-make the world If we think that we can re-make the world as it is to-day, it logically follows that some other man before us has made the world as it is to-day That conclusion frees humanity from all spiritual bondage It strikes at the root of the religious mode of thought (It eliminates the necessity of faith. The classical idealistic philosophy has destroyed religion, but had ended in some sort of Fatalism Pre-Marxian philosophy was essentially fatalistic) Man was a victim of his environments; he had no hand in shaping these environments, and yet all he does and thinks is determined by them That means the whole world is only a vast prison house without an escape, ruled by a God who previously was considered to be spirit, and was now conceived of as matter But in Marxian philosophy man assumes the function of the God What Marx said was not propounded as a dogma But in the light of scientific research he proved that man lives in certain environments, that his behaviour, his being and becoming is determined by these environments But at the same time, man reacts on those environments and shapes them by his reactions He is not an actor on the stage walking over it, detached and untouched, a prescribed route But he is a part of the stage itself His movements are determined by his environments inasmuch as these include his own being. Thus he has become not only the maker and master of his environments including his own self, but he has become the maker of history That is the essence of Marxism

This materialistic interpretation of history enabled Marx to re-write the history of human development Until then, history had been recorded as legend It was a chaotic chronology of facts, and even as facts they are not always authentic Somebody wrote that sometime, somewere there was a battle. Somebody wrote it, and I have to believe it as he wrote it But who can guarantee that that battle really took place, and took place exactly as he described it ? Before Marx gave us the clue to history, even historical knowledge was not knowledge, but a faith Certain things are written in a book, we read them and accepted them But Marx showed that history is also a science to be investigated, requiring research Just as in the physical world, nothing takes place without a cause, similarly in history, in the process of human development, everything that happens is determined by a cause, is the result of previous events. There is nothing arbitrary in history. And Marx gives us the clue with the help of which we can discover the fundamental law of history. That law is that man's ideas are determined not by his environments as such, but by the mode of production through which he earns his livelihood. Here the spiritual being of man is causally connected with his physical being The mode with which he maintains his physical existence determines all the other parts of his existence When he begins with one mode of production, he is not limited by that. He can change it. A porter is not bound to be a porter for eternity. The same power that enables man to manufacture a primitive hammer, eventually enables him to manufacture a hydraulic or an electric hammer The new instrument changes the mode of production, and thereby his entire existence changes In course of the development of higher and higher developed tools and modes of production man's ideas also change. And those changes are the spring of all social evolution

Now having ascertained this fundamental law of history, Marx analysed the social environments in which he lives, and they were the so-called capitalist system He proved that everything in this system, culture, art, human behaviour etc was determined by the capitalist mode of production He further proved that all the human values, the mode of thought and all other spiritual attainments of humanity achieved during the previous periods of history, had been determined by another mode of production which was called the feudalist mode of production Further he discovered that the rise of the capitalist mode of production had contradicted the feudalist mode of production, which had exhausted its possibilities, and while germinating within the old system, the capitalist mode outgrew the frame and had to destroy it, in order to create the superstructure, cultural and otherwise necessary for and corresponding to the conditions of the capitalist mode of production. Finally, Marx came to the conclusion that these changes are re-curring in history, that up to our days, history is nothing but the history of these recurring changes And since these changes have been brought about by man before, there is no reason to believe that such changes will not be brought about by man again if history is not to come to an end If capitalist culture, art, ideas, behaviour etc had to replace previous modes of thought and forms of society, so also capitalist society will be replaced eventually by a new form of society, with a new mode of production, and with a new superstructure of human values, culture, art, ideas, behaviours etc

These are the essential features of Marxian philosophy What we call Marxist economic or political doctrines, follows from that If we want to apply Marxism in politics, we must understand first what is Marxism. One of the fundamental principles of Marxism is that everything happens only if there is an adequate cause. Man's activities, his will, his desires are determined by the social environments in which he lives. Now, in our politics, we hear much of Communism and Socialism and of classless society These are very bright ideals. Some people think, in order to be Marxists, we must believe in those ideals and dream of those ideals But that is not enough. And if we cannot do anything more than that about our ideals, then we may call ourselves Marxists, but we shall not be Marxists In order to be Marxists, we must act. In order to act properly, we must analyse what are the conditions in which we are living and under which we have to act (We have the capacity to remake these conditions, but our desire and will are also limited by those conditions) This is the lesson the progressive intellectuals in our country must learn from Marxism The teaching of Karl Marx is that you cannot make history to order. Therefore, if we want to re-make our society, we shall have to operate with the material that is existing here If we want to create a new form of society, we can only create that form of society the germs of which are already existing in the present form of society It is believed that, in order to be a Marxist, one can not think of another form of society than the Socialist one But Marx only says that Socialism will follow necessarily from the capitalist form of society He says that as far as we can see in the light of the knowledge accessible to us, we can visualise the development of human society to the stage of Communism It does not follow therefrom that human development will stop there Only we have not enough to predict what will be the subsequent form of development. But Marx clearly said that Communism will necessarily follow from Capitalism. Capitalism itself is a pre-supposition of Socialism. So, if we have Capitalism in our country Socialism or Communism will follow as a necessity If we come to the conclusion that the immediate stage in our development will not be Socialist because the indispensable pre-conditions are not existing, that in order to establish Socialism, we have to go through another stage establishing these pre-conditions, then we can be Marxists and with a clear conscience participate in the process of establishing these indispensable pre-conditions without which Socialism can never be built Karl Marx himself, while he wrote the Communist Manifesto, knowing that Communism was to come only when Capitalism had exhausted all its possibilities, in his practical activities actually participated in a political movement for the overthrow of Feudalism and the establishment of Capitalism, of bourgeois, not Socialist society

The habit of identifying Marxism with Communism is erroneous The perspective and the program of Communism results from Marxism But Marxism is greater than Communism Marxism includes not only Communism, but every phase of human development If to-day I am transported to a social environment where the objective process of development is from original primitive Communism to private property, it will not at all be necessary for me to forget my Marxism and my perspective of classless society, to actively participate wholeheartedly in that process of the necessary establishment of private property Because, once I am there, that process is my environment and I have to participate in the development, in the shaping of my environment But being a Marxist, having a wider perspective, knowing how the development will go on after the immediate stage of the given process is reached, I shall be in a position to expedite that process, to promote that process consciously and straight in the necessary direction

But that aspect of Marxism is not appreciated by many in our country That is because there is little knowledge of the real nature of Marxism If we appreciate Marxism as a system of rationalistic, logical, materialistic thought rather than a bunch of dogmas, we shall see that we can be very good Marxists and at the same time have regard for the realities in which we are placed If we do not have regard for those realities, we cannot be good Marxists, because the conclusions regarding the subsequent development will be based on mistakes and we shall not be in a position to rightly estimate and expedite the necessary next stage of the process, that is going on.

I shall conclude by summarising in the following terms. Marxism is not a dogma. A Marxist is not required to believe in a set of certain things Marxism is a philosophy of life, and life is not only the life of a Communist, but also the life of a bourgeois. If we say life, we mean life from the dawn of human evolution to an endless process Marxism does not know any finality. Therefore it is not necessary for us even to abide by the letters of what Marx has written By applying the method which is the essence of Marxism, it will be perfectly legitimate for us, nay, it will be the duty of every Marxist, to elaborate, amplify and even revise Marxism if in the light of the knowledge of modern science, which was not available at the time of Karl Marx, this becomes necessary. Human mind, human knowledge did not stop growing since the three volumes of the "Capital" were written Since Karl Marx wrote, human knowledge has progressed, and if by applying the principle of Marxism, we find that in the light of this knowledge, Marx's teachings have to be amplified, or certain conclusions at which he arrived have to be modified, we shall be bad Marxists if we do not have the courage to do so

You know of the revolutionary discoveries of modern physics They are so very revolutionary that a number of leading physicists have declared that the foundation of Materialism has been knocked out, so that we have to revert to the method of metaphysical speculation and worship at the shrine of some mathematical God If we would stick to the letters of

Marxian materialism, we shall find that we are not in a position to meet the arguments put forth by these modern scientists, because certain scientific knowledge of his time has proved to be fallacious and new facts have been discovered In the days of Marx, matter was conceived of as so many physical entities Modern physics has destroyed that conception So, if you would stick to the letter of Marx's conclusions, you may have the satisfaction of being the most orthodox of all Marxists, but you are not a Marxist according to Marx's own ideas Because you cannot then have a scientific explanation of the world any longer To-day, a Marxist is required to question the fundaments of materialism itself in order to keep pace with the discoveries of modern knowledge

Now, if you concern yourselves with the practical problems before us to-day, you will see that you cannot follow literally the line predicted by Marxism This line was deduced from the analysis of the European situation, from the knowledge of European social systems The analysis of Chinese or Indian systems did not enter into Marx's writing simply because they were not known in Europe at his time So, we can not say that developments here in India must necessarily follow the same line as Marx predicted for European developments Even the present events in

Europe tend to show that things do not always develop straightly and exactly as Marx visualised New factors have arisen which he could not foresee and which react on the line of development So, if this is so in Europe, where Marx lived and which he knew better than anybody else, to maintain that his predictions must serve as prescriptions for the process of development here, is insanity, but not Marxism

It is a very encouraging sign that Marxism is gaining favour in our country It is all the more welcome to me, because(I happen to be one of the pioneers of Marxist propaganda in this country) But it pains me that many are not realising the far-reaching implications of Marxism They do not take pains to understand and study Marxism, but simply behave like parrots, reading a few books and repeating phrases learned by heart And everybody who does not repeat those phrases literally, is a counter-revolutionary Now that is not Marxism As a Marxist, you should be prepared to admit the revolutionary rôle of the bourgeoisie at a certain stage of human development According to Marx, Capitalism is a revolutionary force at a certain stage of development. But to many people in this country, the term bourgeoisie is equal to counter-revolutionary It remains, however, to be seen whether Capitalism in our country can still play the rôle of a progressive force, elevating the entire cultural level of society If we find that this is so, we would have to call Capitalism a revolutionary force, and we shall do so even if Capitalism has become a counter-revolutionary force in England and Germany I do not say that this is so But I say that, if we would find that it is so, we must have the courage as Marxists to admit it

But the usual vulgarisation of Marxism is not altogether our fault It is the fault of our heritage We are proud to be a nation of believers But every nation was once a nation of believers. Only we have continued to be so three hundred years longer than other nations did And the quality of believers is common also to our young Indian Marxists They have turned their back on their belief in Manu, and laid their confidence at the shrine of Saint Marx For an orthodox Indian, whatever Manu wrote two thousand years ago, is immutable, is eternal and infallible and above questioning Now, for a Marxist, Manu was a revolutionary in his days, what-ever may be the value of his teachings for us at present. So, the teachings of Marx are revolutionary teachings. But whether they can be applied in India exactly in the form as they were applied in Germany or England or elsewhere, that we shall have to see, Marxism gives us the liberty to vary these applications As a matter of fact, it puts us the task of varying its application according to the condition to which it has to be applied.

My final word is, if you want to grasp the real meaning of Marxism and apply it to the real problems of the life to-day, you will have to begin studying not from the nineteenth, but from the sixteenth century. We cannot understand Marxism except in the light of its historical background The foundation of Marxism is Rationalism Marxism was the outcome of what is known as the Renaissance movement in Europe. European humanity broke away from the mediaeval mode of thought and groped in darkness for three hundred years Ultimately it evolved a system of philosophy known as Marxism. Without the pains of development in those three hundred years, there would have been no Marx and no Marxism Marxism is the systematisation of all human knowledge developed in those three hundred years If you examine Marxism closely, you will not find anything altogether new. The causal interpretation of history, for intance, was given by other people before Marx Take such a famous popular work as Gibbon's "Decline and Fall of the Roman Empire", It was written long before Karl Marx lived, and you find there a true application of Marxism to the interpretation of history. Marxism was the culmination of a process of thought, of a line of intellectual development that took place in Europe from the sixteenth to the nineteenth century.) I do not say that we shall have to go through all the phases of these hundred years in Europe. But we shall have to understand these phases, we shall have to have the foundation here that was laid in Europe through these three hundred years. If we have not got that foundation, we do not know what is Marxism. And if we yet talk Marxism, without really understanding it, we only transform Marxism into a bunch of dogmas. And if we transform Marxism into a bunch of dogmas, then we do not act as Marxists, but we massacre Marxism.

If you study the history of Indian philosophy, you will find the analogous origin of materialist thought in our country. Between Democritos and Epicuros and Marx, there was a continuous line of development, tracing which Marx could only come to his conclusions. Similarly, there must be stages and phases in our philosophical history between our ancient philosophers and the most modern philosophy of Marxism. You will have to begin your study farther back. Great revolutions, philosophical, intellectual, spiritual and political revolutions took place in Europe before the days of Karl Marx. And we, living in a more backward age than were the days of Karl Marx, shall have to learn from those revolutions. We shall have to understand the ideologies, the character and the social outcome of those revolutions have still to be achieved in our country Those modes of thought which were decisive for those revolutions, which gave a spiritual and moral sanction to those necessary radical transformations in Europe, we must have them here also, in order to bring about a situation in which, eventually, Marxism will be appreciated as it is, when there will be a considerable section of the people prepared to practise Marxism A Marxist in our country, to-day, must appear on the scene as the pioneer of those modes of thought, that is as the pioneer of a Renaissance movement in India He must come forward as a champion of that philosophical revolution, of those transformations of society which preceded Marxism and which ushered in Marxism as a necessary form of human thought

If you speak of Marxism, it will be very easy to go and convince a number of educated young men who have a certain sense of justice, that the workers are being exploited and that Capitalism must be overthrown. But as long as those youngmen remain under the spiritual and religious modes of thought, as it is generally to-day, in action you will always find them lacking If we cannot come to the understanding on the fundamentals, if there is not the full conviction that man is the master of the world, that there is no greater force than human force, you cannot make a man a Socialist or a Communist That will be brought about only by spreading Rationalism, by teaching our young intellectuals to adopt a scientific mode of thought. We are still by and large metaphysically inclined If you try to impose Marxism on metaphysics, you will create a very incongruous thing Therefore, in my opinion today in our country, Marxism can have a force in its essential feature, as a philosophy, because it indicates which revolution has to take place, and which are the pre-conditions for this revolution You will find the greatest opposition to Marxism in the philosophical aspect. And the philosophical arguments given against Marxism cannot be met by the doctrines of Marxism itself, but only by those modes of thought which preceded Marxism That is Rationalism Rationalism has dissolved the religious mode of thought in other parts of the world And you have to dissolve the religious mode of thought in India as well You shall have to dissolve the religious conception of life before you can make people accept the materialistic interpretation of life with an intelligent conviction. I cannot understand how a man blissfully ignorant of history, philosophy and science, can take up a book by Karl Marx, read it and say I am a Marxist. That becomes again a belief The working class becomes Socialist by experience. But for an intellectual it is more difficult to become a Marxist than for a camel to go through a needle An intellectual, in order to become intelligently convinced of it, must be thoroughly acquainted with the foundation of Marxism, and that scientific approach to Marxism is seldom made in our country My answer to the question What is Marxism, is meant to make that clear to you If you want to understand what is Marxism, you must begin to find out how Marxism was developed, and why Marxism had become the philosophy of revolution, the philosophy of future humanity .Marxism is Realism, Marxism is Rationalist approach to everything It is the rejection of all faith, even in Marxism. If we are true Marxists, we must have the courage to submit every single sentence written even by Marx himself to a scrutiny in the light of the discoveries of modern science made since then.) Unless we have got a little of that Marxism in our country, any mere talk of Marxism, Socialism and Communism, will do more harm than good

MARXISM AND MORAL PHILOSOPHY

The foundation of Marxian ethics is laid by the dialectics of Hegel and the scientific Humanism of Feuerbach Setting aside the time-honoured religious, theological and metaphysical dogmas, Feuerbach placed the man, of flesh and blood, in the centre of the world, and proceeded to interpret everything including those dogmas themselves, by human standards Marx and Engels replaced Feuerbach's abstract conception of man as a static unit by the dynamic conception of man as a social being, involved in a continuous process of becoming. The Marxian development of Feuerbach's Humanism was the result of a better application of dialectics to the study of historical and social phenomena Feuerbach's critique was all-shattering. Everything appeared in a new light. The human essence of divine conception was laid bare Theological mysteries were revealed as the result of anthropological pre-occupations. The carnal core of religion was discovered Faith was found to be the expression of egoism But there was a fundamental weakness in Feuerbach's philosophy It was in the point of departure The being of a man determines his consciousness and being is governed by its own laws What are these laws? How do they operate? Feuerbach omitted to answer these questions Man explained everything, but the man himself remained unexplained and appeared as an absolute category

Marx maintained that the consciousness of man is, indeed, determined by his physical existence; but the evolution of human thought—the spiritual progress of man—is determined by social conditions which, in their turn, change the conditions of the physical being of man The view of man as an absolute standard irresistibly leads to the conclusion that man must think and act similarly in all ages, under all circumstances. The corollary to this absolute conception is the idea of eternal truth and immutable standards of morality All possible ambiguity about the being of man which determines his consciousness by the following view of man's relation to nature: "By acting on nature outside himself and transforming it man simultaneously changes his own nature" (Marx)

The struggle for existence is conducted by man not as individuals, but collectively. From the dawn of his history, man has been a social being. Therefore, the laws governing man's being and thought are to be sought in his social relations. Exhaustive investigation of history enabled Marx to establish the fact that the consciousness of man, after all is determined by the way he makes his living, since the modes of making his living, and the modes of living itself, change from time to time, the forms of human thought and the modes of expressing it, change correspondingly. Religion, philosophy, ethics, aesthetics, law, are but the variegated forms of an ideological superstructure, built upon the foundation of economic relations among groups of individuals constituting a social organisation.

As soon as man realises that, as a social being, he is the maker of his own fate, he frees himself from the chains of the metaphysical moral philosophy and throws off the tyranny of dogmatic morality. The basic principle of life is neither absolute truth nor abstract goodness. It is change—continuous advance, a process of becoming, in course of which mankind develops spiritually and morally, thanks to the progressively acquired knowledge of the objective truth of existence. Human ideas and ideals have always changed. The cultural history of mankind, is the record of that process of change. With the power derived from scientific knowledge, mankind finds itself in the position to control the process of future development. In the past, social changes took place at random. That gave rise to the ideas of an arbitrary force dictating the events of human existence. Now, social changes can be brought about according to a previously worked out plan. Moral philosophy should so modify itself as to be able to contribute to the plan of social reconstruction of the future of mankind. Only such principles, standards andvalues, as are deduced from collective social experience, can claim general validity and demand general observance without prejudicing common welfare. Concepts must necessarily change as social conditions change.

In its tradional forms with fixed principles and absolute concepts, moral philosophy serves as a line of ideological defence of the established social order. In this role, it gives lie to its own profession; it defends sectional interest against general welfare which demands revolutionary readjustment of social relations, and a relativist, realist conception of morality to justify, indeed to call for, such a change.

The ideas of goodness, right and wrong, just and unjust, constitute the foundation of traditional ethics. But these ideas have never been clearly defined or traced to some rational origin Some reflection reveals how hopelessly cotradictory these ideas are What does not conform with the values cherished by an established social order, is bad from its point of view Thus what is bad for the present, is good for the future. Because, when a social transformation becomes necessary for the welfare of the aggregate, cherished values are disputed, traditional ideas are unsettled, venerable ideals are rejected by the forces striving for the historically necessary transformation,—a process taking place according to the basic principle of life

Man is by nature non-conformist otherwise, mankind would be still living contentedly under the primeval conditions of savagery Therefore, as Hegel put it, it would be more true to say that man is by nature bad, than to repeat the platitudinous dictum that man is by nature good Whenever any section of mankind took a step forward, it violated the established laws of society and the traditional canons of morality An example to the point is the Indian habit of condemning modern civilisation The ideas and ideals of modern civilisation do not conform with the canons and codes of morality appropriate for the maintainance of society in a backward state Therefore, they are bad. But they are good and desirable for those who would be benefitted by the subversion of the reactionary social order

Moral philosophy, revolutionised by the rejection of the notion of absolute values quickens in man the consciousness of the spirit of nonconformity, which is in his very being as the subjective expression of the fundamental principle of life Marxism as a revolutionary philosophy promotes the process of social transformation, necessary for the progress and welfare of mankind, which derives from scientific knowledge the power to shape its own future Therefore, rejection of dogmatic morality is a part of Marxism. It alone is not rejected It crumbles down because Marxism, in the light of scientific knowledge reveals the fictitious and fraudulent nature of the religious and metaphysical sanctions of moral philosophy

Originally, moral philosophy, that of the West at any rate, grew out of the background of antique naturalism Even modern moral philosophy disclaims any direct bearing upon religion The founder of Western moral philosophy, Socrates, was killed for disbelief in the Gods of natural religion At the close of the middle-ages Humanism and rationalist Metaphysics represented the spirit of revolt against dogmatic religion and mystic theology Nevertheless, the abstract concepts and categorical imperatives of moral philosophy, antique as well as modern, derive their absolute authority ultimately from faith. They are traced back to intuition which cannot be further analysed The final, intuitive standards of morality, must be taken for granted. This is a precarious foundation for any system of philosophical thought Therefore, the sanctions for the standard are derived,by implication, if not explicitly, from the reference to some supernatural, metaphysical world.

The founder of moral philosophy was not Socrates himself, but the Platonic Socrates, that is, Socrates as interpreted by his great disiciple who deduced the metaphysical "moral order" from his doctrine of the Logos That metaphysical foundation of the irreligious moral teachings of Socrates become the philosophical cornerstone of Christian theology

India never developed a system of moral philosophy in the strict sense of the term, that is independent of religion The Smritis and Samhitas represent the nearest approach But the codes of individual and social conduct laid down in those Shastras are rather religious injunctions coming from the priest-hood, than moral precepts to indicate a way of individual spiritual elevation which does not lie through its rites and rituals of religion. They are religious laws for the governance of secular affairs.

In the last analysis, the notion of the absolute constitutes the foundation of moral philosophy which sets up fixed universal standards of goodness, justice, virtue etc., which is composed of dogmatic concepts of morality, which lays down categorical imperatives for the guidance of human conduct. Ask any moral philosopher what is good, the sum and substance of whatever and however much he may have to say in answer will be: Good is conformity with the idea of goodness. If you demand a definition of goodness, you will be told that it is an unanalysable intuitive category which cannot be defined. In other words, it is an absolute concept and as such metaphysical. Modern moral philosophy has improved little upon Plato. The mystic notion of the "moral order" is derived from the picture of the world of abstract ideas. It is supposed that man instinctively strives to measure up to the intuitive concepts of morality. If this theoretical position is consistently maintained, every human action should be regarded as moral. But in practice, moral philosophy becomes dogmatic and lays down codes of human conduct. The contradiction between theory and practice is justified with the argument that the conscious mind (intelligence), influenced by environments, obscures man's moral intuition and obstructs the instinctive striving to conform with the "moral order". Thus, goodness though supposed to be inherent in human nature can be actually realised only by those who can rise above their environments. The final appeal is to prophets and seers Goodness is a reflected light which shines only upon pure souls

Kant made a great effort to place ethics upon a rational foundation But his doctrine of a priori categorical imperative is essentially not different from the traditional Platonic view of the True, the Good and the Beautiful—the view that regards this famous trinity of ethics and aesthetics as absolute values in themselves which transcend the limitations of phenomenal beings, namely, space, time and causality The world of moral law and freedom of will could not hang in the air It must be referred back to something This was realised by moral philosophers of the Kantian school Jacobi, for example, admitted that the final appeal must be to a super-personal principle The core of the "rationalist" metaphysical moral philosophy can be stated as follows The end of philosophy is to know that we must believe. The Kantian school actually did come to this conclusion. The ultimate basis of moral philosophy is thus exposed as the belief in a transcendental world, of abstract values In other words, the conception of the metaphysical "moral order" is but a variation of the conception of the teleological order

The whole structure of moral philosophy collapses in consequence of the discovery that absolute truth is a fiction,—an empty concept This revolutionary discovery is made in the revealing light of modern scientific knowledge. Marxism is its philosophical outcome.

The structure was a castle built in the air. Moral values are not absolute, they are relative. What is good for one may not be good for another. Indeed, it may be, it often is, positively bad for others Their validity is temporally variable also What is good for today may not be good tomorrow. All the concepts of moral philosophy are equally relative. The notion of "values in themselves" is even more bizarre than the notion of "things in themselves" By undermining the religious and metaphysical foundation of this notion, science revolutionises moral philosophy which apparently does not seem to have any bearing upon the facts and events of the physical world

Humanism represents an ineffective effort to overthrow the tyranny of dogmas claiming supernatural sanction To end that tyranny, exercised through moral philosophy as well as religion, supernatural fictions must be replaced by the objective, empirical, verifiable truths of nature as the guides to human behaviour, as standards of human conduct Humanism does not do this. It disputes supernatural authority; but places the abstract "man" above nature. The situation is hardly improved when the fiction of God is replaced by the fantasy of the abstract conception of man divorced from the special, temporal, historical and social environment which make man what really he is, in each given period of history or even in each given movement of individual life "Human nature as something eternal, unchangeable, essentially or instinctively good, has no more objective reality than the immortal soul, divine will or the metaphysical "moral order"

Man can throw off the tyranny of the supernatural, of the mysteries of the metaphysical, only with the power derived from the knowledge that he is a part of the physical world To be philosophically effective, Humanism must be naturalistic, not ethical Man, with all his mental, emotional and spiritual make-up, being an integral part of the physical Universe, human nature is changeable as all other aspects of nature Therefore, the mystic conception of eternal and unchangeable human nature cannot serve as the final standards of value must also change The slightest critical acquaintance with the history of social evolution compels the rejection of the notion that human nature is unchangeable

Moral standards change from time to time, from place to place according to the physical environments and social conditions in which man lives. Man is a social animal; his nature is determined by whatever he does, or is compelled to do, for the maintenance and welfare of the social aggregate Human society is not a static organisation It grows and changes The means and modes of its existence and conditions for the promotion of collective welfare change influencing man's moral outlook accordingly Man has no individual being outside and independent of his social relations He realises his individuality as a member of the aggregate The collective does not bear the stamp of individuals composing it On the contrary, the individual is determined by the conditions of the society in which he lives. Man is the sum total of historical and social experience Moral philosophy, in the last analysis, is social philosophy Moral codes are determined by social necessities The standard of values is the welfare of the aggregate

Moral philosophy refers its precepts and principles to abstract, mystic, metaphysical concepts such as goodness - in - itself, when it is actuated, consciously or not, by the concern for the maintenance of an established social order based upon sectional interest which militates against the welfare of the entire community The sanction for an immoral social order is found in the imaginary "moral order" which, in its turn, is ultimately interpreted as the expression of the divine will. An immutable absolute "moral order" presupposes the teleological order: The world is so, because it could not be otherwise, being the product of providential design.

Marxism separates morality from all this mystic, metaphysical context. It enables men to behave morally not under compulsion, but by his own choice and voluntary submission to the laws made for the welfare of the entire community The fundamental principle of Marxian ethics can be stated in the words of Epicurus who exclaimed: "I want to be free from the tyranny of the Gods, so that I could be virtuous because it gives me pleasure to be virtuous."

THE CULT OF NON-VIOLENCE:

ITS SOCIO-POLITICAL SIGNIFICANCE.

The introduction of non-violence into a political struggle is proclaimed not only as the token of Gandhiji's greatness, but also as the characteristic contribution of India's special genius to the solution of the problems of the modern world. But intellectual independence does not permit the acceptance of a doctrine on its face value, simply because it is backed with the name of a great man or by the authority of some mystic racial peculiarity Even when the great man is also a good man, the goodness of the doctrine can not be taken for granted Internal logic is the acid test of all doctrines and propositions. They should be judged by their implications, and that again not abstractly, but from the point of view of human welfare, social utility. Man is a social animal; therefore, a socially injurious doctrine, however lofty abstractly, can never be conducive to human welfare, spiritual as well as material

None except those whose moral senses are totally paralysed, as the Fascist war-mongers, for instance, advocates violence for the sake of violence It is a loathesome heritage of the barbarous past of mankind But to abhor violence is entirely different from making a moral dogma or religious cult of non-violence, to be practised absolutely, even when the great bulk of mankind groans under violence The cult, however laudable abstractly, is irreligious and immoral, because, while preaching non-violence, it actually condones the practice of violence

The creed of non-violence has compelled the Congress to waive the right of using all means for attaining Swaraj Consequently, the professed ideal remains an ideal never to be realised Arbitrary limitation of the means puts the end beyond reach Congress leaders can be easily compelled to make the damaging confession that, if the attainment of political independence be ever found to be conditional upon the use of violence, they would have to forego independence, since they are committed to the creed of non-violence. Incidentally, it is hereby also confessed that they are not committed to the ideal of independence. That commitment is conditional, and does not impose upon them any binding moral responsibility Pure political consideration, of course, cannot have much weight for those primarily concerned with an ethical creed, buttressed ultimately on religious faith Since unconditional adhesion to the creed of non-violence must have priority over the exigencies of the struggle for political freedom, in the last analysis, the cult of non-violence amounts to conformity with imperialist violence

It is hardly necessary to argue the point that the imperialist domination of any country is a system of organised violence For the moment, only a few words will suffice The legality of the Imperialist State is ultimately founded upon the right of conquest, which is an act of violence The admission that political independence might not be attained by non-violent means, is compelled by the realisation of the fact that violence bars the way to the goal To forego the goal upon that realisation is to admit that the imperialist practice of violence is morally more justifiable than a subject people's right to political independence Those who really believe in the morality of this right, can never forego it; because that would be betrayal of a moral principle - an immoral act. If you are really convinced of the morality of your right, you should have no moral scruple against the assertion of the sacred right of revolt in pursuance of your conviction. The cult of non-violence has prevented the Congress from thinking out consistently the implications of its curious ideology.

The social significance of the cult is positively sinister. A little analysis would reveal that Let us take a declaration made by the prophet of the cult, in an unguarded moment. Some time in 1934, Gandhiji was interviewed by one Mr. Lotwalla, in behalf of some American journal. Answering a question about his attitude toward the Indian Princes, Gandhiji said that, if ever any attempt was made to expropriate them violently, he would defend their position by all means. For defending the right of the Princes, he would employ all means, which evidently include violence. A subject people should rather forego the incontestably moral, and therefore legal, right to freedom, if in pursuit of that goal they would be compelled to assert the right of revolt, the sacredness of which has been proclaimed by history and admitted by all the great moralists and jurists of the modern world. But for the defence of the ugly relics of barbarism, which constitute stout links in the chain of India's slavery, the use of violence is morally permissible !

This is really not so far-fetched as it may appear to the uncritical. It is the logical conclusion of

Gandhiji's own statement. He must have known what he was talking about, he is noted for frankness and sincerity. Everything he says is to be believed; his sincerity is not to be questioned So one cannot be blamed of extravagance for drawing the obviously logical conclusion from a statement deliberately made by him.

However, one can approach the problem from another side, and yet arrive at the same conclusion. Let us do a bit of experimenting with truth. Gandhiji would not approve of any violent attack upon the Princes. He is not concerned with their mundane interests, but with the spiritual principle of non-violence. The object of his defense is not the privileges of the Princes, but the creed of non-violence, which is so very dear to him that he would resort to violence to defend it! Let us dismiss the incredible eventuality of his actually leading an army to defend feudal barbarism But having done that, we are still left with a fact which exposes the sinisterness of the creed of non-violence

Even the most ardent apologists of the Princes would find it very difficult to prove that those pampered parasites perform the function of benevolent fathers of their subjects None would suggest that the régime in the Indian States is based upon voluntary contract between the rulers and the ruled. The régime is based upon coercion, which implies violence, actual or potential Absolute adhesion to the creed of non-violence makes one a passive, if not active, defender of this règime of violence. Any attempt to clear away the stinking debris of an immoral system is not morally permissible, if it entails the use of violence which would not be done voluntarily, but as a matter of compulsion. For, the system to be abolished would naturally defend itself, and not have any scruple as regards the means to be employed in the defense of selfish interest As a matter of fact, the system is maintained by force But it is morally permissible to let millions and millions of human beings be subjected to standing violence !

The choice is not between violence and non-violence; it is between violence and violence — between violence practised for ages, for enslaving, exploiting, tyrannising multitudes of human beings, and a possible, obligatory use of violence for the liberation of these slaves, for the assertion of human rights, for the sacred cause of freedom, for putting an end to violence. The cult of non-violence represents voluntary choice of the former form of violence It defends the practice of violence, while professing the creed of non-violence.

Believers in the creed argue that the fact that any given system is maintained by violence, does not justify the employment of violence by the victims of the system, even if they cannot be liberated otherwise. The most charitable characterisation of this attitude would be defeatism, which itself is essentially no better than sheer cowardice. In reality, it is something still worse. It is passive support to the perpetuation of the enslavement of the multitude.

Absolute ruling out of the use of violence in the struggle for political and social freedom, could be pressed, consistently with an unswavering adhesion to the cause of freedom and loyalty to the principles of morality, only if the advocates thereof were able to prove that the emergency would never arise. This they cannot do; because there are two parties involved in the struggle, and the choice of weapon is dictated by the party in power. As the advocates of absolute non-violence do not really believe that they would ever be able to persuade the party in power to forego the use of force, on which its very existence depends, they cannot honestly guarantee that the emergency would never arise. Therefore, at the critical moment they would prefer surrender, to the adhesion to the cause of freedom. They may find satisfaction in experimenting with a philosophy which, despite its apparent moral excellence, represents passive endorsement of the servitude of the masses. But the realist cannot fail to see the sinister implication of the cult, which cannot stand the test of a critical analysis. Let the preachers of non-violence persist in their effort to avoid the use of violence in the struggle for freedom; they shall have the support and sympathy of all civilised human beings Let them have the illusion of changing the heart of the heartless oppressors and exploiters of the masses But if they demand that the enslaved multitude must never use force, even when there would be no other alternative, when they would be compelled to choose between the exercise of the sacred right of revolt and abject submission to slavery, then the prophets of non-violence lay themselves open to the charge of betraying the ideal they profess For, in that case, with all their spiritual ideals, moral dogmas and humanitarian professions, in practice, they serve the interests of the oppressor and exploiter Those who actually serve Mammon, cannot serve God. The cult of non-violence supports the practice of violence for the perpetuation of an immoral, vulgar, materialistic system

Gandhiji's secretary once issued an indignant press statement that journalists put into Gandhiji's mouth what he never said. Warned by that statement, let us doubt the authenticity of the report quoted above, though no dementi was issued when it was published. However, granted that he never made the statement, the fact remains that, under the influence of his philosophy and personal guidance, the Congress has adopted the policy of non-interference in the affairs of the Indian States That policy implies recognition of the privileged position of the Princes, and, consequently, approval of the means with which the position is maintained The policy has been justified with all sorts of sophistry and opportunist arguments, which show that it has been adopted deliberately by those responsible for it Bhulabhai Desai's legal defense not only of the feudal political rights, but also of the ceremonial social privileges enjoyed by the parasitic Princes, has not been disowned by the Congress.

It would not do to argue that the Congress has not the power to put its sentiments for the States' peoples into practice, because it failed to do even so much as could be always done, namely, to frame its political programme in accordance with the professed social idea and to strive for the realisation of that programme. Since, the declared policy of the Congress implies recognition of the privileges of Princes, it logically follows that it will defend these privileges whenever necessary and the employment of all means is implicit in any scheme of defense. You either defend something, or you do not If you do, you do so by all means. So, granted that Gandhiji never actually made any such statement as reported by the journalist quoted above, he should take up such an attitude if he consistently acted according to the policy he has persuaded the Congress to follow.

In his speech at the Round Table Conference, Gandhiji declared "Above all, the Congress represents the dumb, semi-starved millions, no matter whether they come from British India or what is called Indian India Every interest which, in the opinion of the Congress, is worthy of protection, has to subserve the interest of these dumb millions If there is a genuine, real clash (of interest), the Congress will sacrifice every interest for the sake of the interest of the dumb millions" These are admirable sentiments, the sincerity of which is beyond doubt But the point again is that it is not a question of sincerity, but of logic The humanitarian sentiments of Gandhiji are contradicted and rendered ineffective by his ethical and religious approach to social and political questions. How are the sentiments, expressed in the passage quoted above, to be reconciled with the proclaimed determination to defend the interest of the Princes, or even with the Congress policy of non-intervention ?

The readiness of the Congress to defend the interest of the dumb millions is not so conclusive as it appears to be. It is clearly hypothetical, the condition is "if there is a genuine real clash of interest" But it is not necessary to have a hypothetical programme. The fact is that there is a clash of interest, and in that clash, the Princes in the Indian India and the corresponding exploiting and oppressing classes in British India have the upper-hand, because they depend essentially on the practice of violence The condition, "if there is a genuine real clash", implies that, in the opinion of Gandhiji, no such clash exists, and there is no reason why it should ever take place Now, there is only one way to avoiding the clash breaking out into an open conflict, sooner or later It is to persuade the dumb millions to remain dumb for ever, to be resigned to their lot, and to make a virtue of the resignation which provides the guarantee for the privileges enjoyed by their oppressors and exploiters.

Class struggle can be avoided only by persuading the exploited masses to accept social slavery as a providential arrangement. The religio-ethical cult of non-violence may serve that purpose Given the ideology that in the Indian society there is no real clash of interest, and that there must be social harmony within the framework of the established order, it logically follows that any clash, should it ever break out, is to be regarded as not "genuine", but artificially fomented by perverse advocates of violence. For the preservation of the traditional social relations, which alone are believed to guarantee harmony and inspire higher ideals of life, the disturbing spirit and its manifestations should be suppressed. The result would be, defense of the established order by all means, should the victims of this order, that is, the dumb millions, ever try to overthrow it by force And the world would be presented with the gratifying spectacle of violence practised for the defense of the principle of non-violence Whoever, on dogmatic moral ground, debar the use of force in the struggle for the liberation of the oppressed, even when the goal is otherwise unattainable, are always practising violence or conniving at the practice, for the suppression of the masses There is absolutely no logical ground for belief that our orthodox Congressmen would behave differently. Their action will be determined by their ideology, which invokes high moral principles and religious sanctions for the justification of a social order which guarantees to a minority privileges at the expense of the majority

This short exposition of the real significance of the cult of non-violence will be best concluded by a reference to the latest pronouncement of the prophet of the cult. In an article called "Is Violence creeping in ?", Gandhiji writes in the 'Harijan'.

"To prevent workers from going to their work by standing in front of them, is pure violence and must be given up The owners of the mill or other factories would be fully justified in invoking the assistance of the police, and a Congress Government would be bound to provide it, if the Congressmen concerned would not desist .....The Congress, which aims at securing full justice for the famishing millions, cannot favour Capitalism But the Congress, so long as it retains non-violence as its basic policy, cannot resort to usurpation, much less allow any class of persons to be insulted or humiliated in any way whatsoever, or allow any Congressman or a body of Congressmen to take the law in their own hands "

Any comment is hardly necessary. When a Congress Government will find it necessary to send the police for dispersing workers picketting a factory, it will obviously order commission of violence on the pretext of defending the abstract principle of non-violence Despatching the police for dispersing a group of people entails the authorisation to do so by all means, including the use of firearms. And for what purpose should the defenders of non-violence go to that extent ? To prevent that the Capitalists are in any way inconvenienced, insulted or humiliated! No wonder that Congressmen in office are behaving like those who came to scoff, but stayed to pray. The creed of non-violence has converted them into stalwart defenders of the imperialist law and order.

SCIENCE AND PHILOSOPHY

Philosophy has always speculated about the nature of the substratum of the world One of the primitive questions that stimulated philosophical thought was, what is the world made of ? Cosmological speculation began with the question, how things happen. The question, obviously, pre-supposes the existence of something in which changes take place, and that these changes constitute the world of experience Thus, the notion of substance is one of the fundamental concepts of philosophy In the last analysis, it is the most fundamental concept The distinction between the substance and its property was inherent in the concept. From that distinction rose the antithetical ideas, such as, form and content, phenomenon and nomenon, appearance and reality, which confused philosophy throughout its history

The latter doctrine of primary and secondary qualities of substance was yet another outcome of the speculative nature of the most fundamental concept of philosophy. On the rise of modern natural science, the function of examining the properties of matter was allotted to it That was the task science modestly set to itself The problem regarding the nature of substance was still left for philosophy to solve. Eventually, philosophy solved the problem by denying the very existence of substance

The modesty of science was a mere formality. As a matter of fact, modern natural science gradually transformed the notion of substance from a vague speculative concept to an inductive generalisation. Concrete knowledge about its properties put definite content into the concept of substance

Originally, philosophy, guided by commonsense, had conceived the sub-stratum of the world as a material entity—qualitatively similar to the world of experience But, in course of time, that original commonsense, realist conception, was supplanted by mystic, metaphysical notions The differentiation between properties and essence was so much emphasised as to transform the latter into an immaterial category, and even the materiality of the former was but grudgingly condemned To distinguish appearances from the reality, properties from essence, came to be the whole of philosophy The metaphysical, the mysterious, the absolute became the sole concern of philosophy. It disdainfully refused to take notice of flitting appearances, of the phenomenal world It believed to have solved the problem of the sub-stratum of the world, only the sub-stratum of its imagination had nothing in common with the world of experience. Yet, the problem had originally risen out of the question, what is the world made of? Thus, the solution was no solution Baffled by its fundamental problem, philosophy had simply gone off in a speculative tangent, away from the road to the discovery of the concrete nature of the sub-stratum of the world of experience

Modern natural science took up the investigation which alone could lead to a relevant reply to the fundamental question of philosophy Virtually, it took over the function which philosophy had failed to perform Nor was science altogether unconscious of its real significance For a long time, physics called itself natural philosophy The immediate result of the new approach to the fundamental problem of philosophy was, indeed, not its final solution; but it was a revolution in the concept of substance, rather revival of the original notion that the sub-stratum of the world is material.

Philosophy had wandered away from its original position. It had dismissed nature as a shadow, and had soared up on the giddy height of the super-natural reality. It had built its fine castle in the thin air of imagination. The revolution in the concept of substance, brought about by modern natural science, though an important development in the history of philosophy, nevertheless meant repudiation of all metaphysical speculation which until then had passed as philosophy Philosophy retaliated by denying the very existence of substance It was a curious sort of defence,—to blast its own foundation ! But philosophy had built itself a beautiful castle in the thin air which, by its very nature, did not require any foundation On the contrary, a material substance would soil the beauty of the picture of its imagination

The philosophical reaction inaugurated by Berkeley represented an order for science to liquidate itself The function allotted to science was only to examine the properties of things If things did not exist, the question of examining their properties could not arise at all But with all its respect for philosophy, modern natural science was not prepared to commit suicide at the old dame's behest. It has risen as a victorious revolt against religious philosophy, and represented the re-birth of true philosophy. When scared by the re-appearance of material substance, philosophy denied the very existence of things, its fundamental problem became the problem of physical science. In course of its development, physical research encroached upon the traditional preserves of philosophy. Finally, it has solved the fundamental problem of philosophy If curiously, the solution is still called the problem, that is due to the habit of differentiating between the functions of science and philosophy

Physics has acquired a mass of exact knowledge about the sub-stratum of the world It knows what it is made of; that is to say, it has found the answer to the question with which philosophy originally started on its eventful career Why do some physicists still insist upon being neutral as regards the question of substance? The answer to this puzzling question is to be found in the new terms, "operationalism" and "functionalism" The function of science is traditionally considered to be to examine the properties of things; therefore, scientific knowledge, however comprehensive, should not claim to do more than describe the properties of things themselves The problem which some physicists would hand over to philosophy, however, is not the old problem It is a mere problem of formalism which grew out of the habit of differentiating between the properties and essence of things. Science inherited this habit from philosophy, and it is out of sheer habit (when no other motive is involved) that some physicists would have philosophy abolish the distinction. The old problem is solved, but philosophy is asked to take the credit

But there is a joker in the game. As far as physical research is concerned, independent of personal predilections of individual physicists, it does not leave any choice for philosophy. The problem is handed over, but not the choice to solve it this way or that The solution is forced, because there is no longer any room for calculation about the nature of substance. Philosophy has got to recognise in the result of modern physical research the description of things it vaguely conceived It has to get over the old habit of distinguishing between the thing and its properties. It has to realise that properties are not attached to something which presumably exists in an expropriated state, so to say; that the term "property" is misleading Thought and search for knowledge will be very much simplified if the concept of "property" is abandoned For example, so much confusion would be avoided by saying that water freezes under certain conditions, instead of saying that it has the property of freezing. The alternative statement is equally explicit, but obviates the necessity of distinguishing between water and its property to freeze The distinction is not necessary. The property to freeze does not exist by itself. On the other hand, the thing 'water' is this property plus others The thing is the sum total of what is called its properties These, therefore, can be regarded only as abstracted behaviours or functions of the thing under specific circumstances Scientific research has accumulated all the empirical data and formulated the necessary theoretical argumentations in the light of which philosophy can abolish the differentiation between the essence and properties of things And this abolition, which indeed will be nothing more than getting over an old habit, is the remaining step towards the solution of the fundamental problem of philosophy, the problem of substance

Philosophy originally wanted to find out, what was the world made of. The desire was to reduce natural phenomena to a basis of unity—to find unity in diversity The philosophical concept of a common sub-stratum was speculative In various forms, it was assumed as the basis for the explanation of natural phenomena without introducing super-natural agencies Science started from the other end. Instead of explaining the world on the strength of a hypothetical common sub-stratum, it started with actual things which composed the world of experience. That was, obviously, the surest way to the discovery of what the world was ultimately made of Science analysed the world step by step, down to its ultimate constituents, and has reduced the number of these to the most minimum. The underlying unity is well within sight

Brought actually face to face with the unitary sub-stratum of the phenomenal world, philosophy can no longer retain the dualist notion of essence and property It must admit that, having analysed all the properties of substance, that is to say, having discovered how the substance behaves or functions under changing conditions, physical research has revealed the nature of substance If there does not seem to be anything tangible at the back of the properties, functions and relations described by physics, that is because properties are not hitched on to something mysterious, because while these are described the thing itself is described Physical research has experimentally exposed the emptiness of the concept of nomenon. It cannot say anything about the thing-in-itself, simply because no such category exists, except as an abstraction

The phrase " content of reality " is either meaningless or tendencious. It is a different formulation of the old doctrine of reality and appearance.

If a content of the reality of physical research is postulated, then the reality is implicitly degraded to the level of mere appearance Or we are asked to visualise two realities—an unnecessary multiplication of categories If something is real, then it is real and that means it can exist by itself If physics deals with reality, then the question of " content " does not arise The physics, then, is meaningless It is tendencious because it hints about some higher reality behind the physical reality, not accessible to scientific research One is at liberty to believe in such higher reality, if he is so inclined But the belief certainly does not result from modern physical research The categories of physical research are all measurable entities So, if you want to refer the reality of physical research to its hypothetical content, which is presumably metaphysical, or immaterial, you get involved in a serious logical fallacy You thereby maintain that an immaterial being can be possessed of properties of physical nature If that is so, the higher reality or the metaphysical " content " of physical reality, postulated by you is not immaterial, and if it is not immaterial, it is accessible to physical research, being not qualitatively different from the object of this research. Assuming that it has not yet been discovered, physics can be sure of discovering it in course of time

Physical research has solved the fundamental problem of philosophy, and is challenging philosophy to disown the solution Philosophy cannot do that, because that would mean negation of the idea of substance The sub-stratum of the world has been revealed to be different from the a priori conception of it. But there is no question about its materiality. The term 'material' means that the substance of the world is an objective entity, and further, that its existence is not to be justified on the authority of any higher reality.

The task of philosophy is to find the explanation of nature, including the vital and spiritual phenomena (life, mind, will, emotion, soul etc), in nature itself, without reference to any super-natural category the existence of which cannot be proved, which is beyond experience, unknown and unknowable. To-day science enables philosophy to perform its task, because all processes of nature can be traced down to an ultimate physical state which is self-sufficient That is substance It is not a static, absolute being, but a state of flux. There is no substance as some sort of a formless, inert stuff out of which the world is made. It is an analytical category,—an abstraction. The substance exists in the form of the world of our experience. Since we can never escape this, the notion of substance can never be abandoned Philosophy starts from commonsense, therefore, it cannot do without the concept of substance Only when it leaves nature, and wanders into the imaginary realm of the super-natural, it rejects the idea of material substance But then it ceases to be philosophy, and becomes religion Instead of explaining nature, it mystifies nature Rejection of the concept of substance is associated with the negation of the reality of the physical world Indeed, even religion does not deny substance Negation of the reality of the world as such is not a part of religion The belief in another world—of spirit, or heaven—does not necessarily imply the negation of this The doctrine either of creation or of emanation proves the existence of this, material, world You may prefer the other world of imagination to this, but your preference for the imaginary does not make the real unreal And this world is despised by the religious because it is material

Before it identified itself with religion, ancient philosophy, whenever it attained a sufficiently high level of development, speculated about the basic stuff of the world Atomism was preceded by the notion that in the beginning, there was water or fire or air. Primitive materialism grew not only in ancient Greece, but in India as well. Indian philosophy has not always been spiritualism par excellence The more highly elaborated materialist systems are practically lost, or have come down to us in fragments But the doctrine of five elements was so prevalent that it entered into the whole ancient literature Beside Kanada's atomism, there was Kapila's naturalism The latter analysed nature into twenty-five elements which, significantly enough, included mind and intelligence

Even religion cannot do without the notion of a material substance. God creates the world out of something, and that something, in so far as it is distinct from nothing, is material Since it is the stuff of which physical things are made Of course, the religious believe in creation out of nothing—by the omnipotence of God But that is because they do not analyse their belief If they did, they would not believe

Briefly, nothing short of an outright denial of the very existence of the world as an objective entity can possibly enable philosophy to get rid of the concept of substance. The fact of physical research itself does not permit such denial. And to-day, philosophy cannot disregard that fact. To hold that the postulate of substance is not necessary for knowledge, is to say that one can have knowledge without knowing something. The discovery that matter is not constructed just as it was previously conceived to be, does not affect the existence of matter

From the time of Berkeley, modern philosophy broke away from science and lost sight of substance—its most fundamental concept It got involved in an essentially fallacious epistemology It was absurd to raise the question, how is knowledge possible, after having denied the existence of the object of knowledge. Having dismissed the object of experience, it went on to ascertain the nature of the content of experience! The denial of the sub-stratum led to the negation of the objectivity of the world of phenomena, composed of the qualities of matter Subjective idealism was triumphant. The world was interpreted as the projection of man's mind Berkeley argued that matter as "unknown something" was nothing The argument had force as long as matter was conceived as the substratum of things to which sensible qualities were attached According to that conception, matter itself could not be described, per se, it had no description The qualities are not its qualities Some are "attached" to it, others are "supported" by it Berkeley was right to insist that it was unnecessary to postulate such a category as its reality could never be demonstrated.

To-day Berkeley's arguments have lost all force. His attack was directed against the conception of matter of that time Science has abandoned that conception. Subjective idealist criticism of the concept of substance, therefore, has no point now Properties of matter can be measured, they are measured with a very high degree of accuracy Qualities of matter can be described. The neo-Berkelians of our day cannot get around the fact that properties and qualities, the former, at any rate, do belong to things Therefore, they argue that we know the properties of substance, but not its nature Even if the validity of this argument was granted, it does not have the same force as in the time of Berkeley To-day, the substance can be described, therefore, it cannot be dismissed as unknown something indistinguishable from nothing. It is irrelevant to hang on to the Lockian distinction between the sub-stratum and qualities of things, when exact knowledge of the structure of matter has invalidated the distinction made in the days of backward scientific knowledge

Thus, modern physical research has again placed the concept of substance in the centre of philosophical discussion It has compelled philosophy to come down on earth from the etherial region of vain epistemological speculations — theories about the content of experience based upon the negation of the possibility of experience To-day, there is no doubt about the reality of substance. Its objective existence has been empirically verified When one talks about the nature of a thing, he obviously admits its existence. While proving the objective reality of substance, modern physical research has also revealed its nature. We admit its reality, because we know it, and our knowledge of the objective reality of substance is the sum-total of informations about its properties and qualities. The nature of a thing is expressed by its properties. When they are described, the thing is described.

In the philosophical sense, substance is something that can exist by itself. 'By substance we can conceive nothing else than a thing which exists in such a way as to stand in need of nothing beyond itself in order to exist." (Descartes) This description still holds good, although Descartes' own elaboration of it has turned out to be erroneous. It has been found out that "extension in space" is not an invariant attribute of matter. On the other hand, with the disappearance of the notion of empty space, the expression "extension in space" loses all significance. To put matter to this test now, is to employ an obsolete standard. The original definition remains the crucial test, and matter can stand it more successfully than any other content of the concept of substance. The strength of matter lies in its self-sufficiency, because uniqueness automatically results from self-sufficiency. Something that can exist by itself excludes all other existence. As soon as more than one existence are postulated, either of them ceases to be self-sufficient and unique. There must be relation which necessarily implies inter-dependence. Thus, the content of the concept of substance can be defined as self-sufficiency and uniqueness. Substance is material because only matter can exist by itself. This was not realised in the days of Berkeley and before him In its earlier days, modern natural science visualised matter as an inert mass, which was moved by "force" But since then, the causes of the movement of matter is an established fact All the processes of matter can be explained without assuming the intervention of any extraneous factor Substance could not be equally self-sufficient if it were spiritual. A material world — a reality of lower order — has to be postulated as the vehicle of the spiritual essence If the existence of the physical world is totally denied, then the spiritual reality itself is also annihilated Its existence is proved by material manifestations In the absence of these, the notion of a spiritual essence — of a reality behind shadowy appearances, does not arise Spirit realises itself in matter This may be characterised as unreal, illusory, ignorance, anything you please; but the fact remains that without it, spiritual being remains a non-entity. It is beside the point to assert that it exists in the potential state of absolute being In order to prove that it exists, there must be someone to testify to its existence, and the testimony, whatever may be its value, can come only from man who is a part of physical existence. Then, to be real, being must include becoming, and nothing can become of the spiritual substance except through the intermediary of the material being The assumption that substance is spiritual, leads to dualism, because spirit is nothing in the absence of matter. The unnecessary dualism could be maintained philosophically, so long as matter was conceived as an inert mass which required something to be moved. With our present dynamic conception of matter, dualism has become utterly gratuitous, and monism can only be materialist

Philosophy cannot get away from the fundamental concept of substance, and science proves that substance is material All speculation about the nature of substance is irrelevant to-day You do not speculate about a thing that stands clearly before you The nature of substance is material, because otherwise it would not be substance, it would not be self-sufficient and unique. What does not satisfy these conditions, cannot be the substance of the world Only matter can be and become by itself That is the basic lesson of modern physical research which conclusively demonstrates the materiality of the sub-stratum of the world of experience.

The term "substance" is misleading. Traditionally, it has the significance of "essence". Dualism is implicit in the term Associated with it is the idea that the world of experience is to be distinguished from the something which underlies it or which it is made of. Hence all the speculation about the content of the concept All this unnecessary confusion is ended by substituting the term substance by the term matter. This terminological clarification is justified firstly on the logical consideration set forth above, and secondly, it is warranted by the result of modern physical research Any doubt on this score is finally dispelled when it is realised that the world of the physicist and, therefore, of the philosopher, is not the abstract world of the mathematician The physicist has analysed the world to ultimate units of matter called electron, proton, unit charge of electricity and the quantum of action But this has been done in abstraction The world has not actually been broken up into bits Physical research has not reduced the world to abstractions—"pointer-readings", a bunch of mathematical formulae, etc The world remains a concrete reality The constants of physics are analytical categories. They are physically real because they have been deduced from the real world of experience They are real as constituents of it The scientist starts from this undeniable reality, and gathers knowledge about its structure and laws by isolating its component parts in abstraction. That is also the path of philosophy. Consciousness of, and reaction to, the environments mark the beginning of the process of the enquiry into and the explanation of existence.

The mathematician begins from the other end. The abstract concepts are the material with which he operates Consequently, the world that he constructs with his symbols, is a fiction, but that is not the actual world. Fortunately, the physicist has not actually broken up the world into parts. The mathematician's world is a world of symbols, the physicist, however, stands with his feet on the world of matter. Atoms, protons, electrons, photons, taken out of the context of their real physical, composite, existence, are abstractions. And precisely for that reason, they do not exist. They are fictions. By their very nature, abstractions are not real. An electron is an abstraction, the world is made of electrons, so the world is a construction of the physicist's mind. Thus argues the mathematician But the physicist does not build a world out of electrons. The world is there, he simply analyses it to its ultimate constituent, and says that everything in it is a conglomeration of bits of matter, called electrons. The abstractness of the analytical categories does not in the least affect the concrete physical reality of the world of experience from which they are derived. On the contrary, the reality of this latter logically puts into the abstract concept the content of materiality.

By reducing the physical world to a dynamic unitary sub-stratum, modern scientific research finally solves the philosophical problem of substance. In this situation, it is meaningless to distinguish the essence from its properties It was necessary to postulate an essence of things when the diverse aspects of physical existence were still to be traced to a common foundation This done, the notion of an invariant essence, distinct from changing properties, becomes superfluous. The solution of the problem of substance lies in the disappearance of the dualist conception of things. The traditional notion of substance pre-supposes the existence of a featureless, that is to say, absolute something, to which properties are attached Such a category does not exist; it is a metaphysical abstraction. A wrong formulation — to a large extent of linguistic nature — made the problem of substance so very baffling The substratum of the physical world is not a featureless something to which and in which changes take place, the changes being the changes of the configuration of its properties, not of itself. It is a process of happenings Modern physical research has discovered it to be so This dynamic nature of the sub-stratum of the physical world is described by the electric conception of matter, and the mathematical scheme of wave-mechanics associated with it.

Primordially, matter is not something that exists in space and changes in time It is the sole existence The existence of matter is realised in its transformation into multitudinous patterns The concepts of space and time are derivative categories, representing respectively the geometrical and chronological functions of material existence. Therefore, it is logically fallacious to apply the standards of location and duration to primordial, microcosmic, matter In the absence of matter, there will be neither space nor time It is obviously absurd to make the reality of matter conditional upon its subservience to categories the reality of which depends on the reality of matter. The test of "simple location' is invalidated by empirical facts On the one hand, the theory of relativity shows that there is no such thing as empty space, space is identified with the extendedness of matter On the other hand, quantum physics has analysed matter to basic units identical with the smallest segments of space-time In view of this empirically established identity of the concept of mass (extendedness) and space, the notion of extension in space becomes meaningless. This notion pre-supposes two entities — one extended in the other. The test, obviously, has no application to the unitary sub-stratum of the physical universe which, nevertheless, is material

The real test is infinite extension. If matter is infinitely extended, the possibility of any other extension is precluded. In that case, everything existing must be regarded as material The notion of extension in space deprives matter of infinity It is not logically compulsory to assume that something that extends in space, fills up the entire space Indeed, the notion of extension in space is inseparably associated with the atomist conception of matter, and this conception leaves empty space which limits the extension of matter Therefore, the fact that primordially, matter transcends the notion of extension in space only proves that its extension is not limited, it is infinite, precluding the possibility of any other existence Primordially, matter is not extended in space, because its extension, physical existence, is not limited It is the only existence, and as such does not require anything else as the condition for its existence Thus, matter is fully qualified to occupy the position of the philosophical category of substance Its qualification is certified by modern physics.

The result of modern physical research does not leave any room for the speculation about the nature of substance It abolishes the notion of a "substance". It reveals the structure of the sub-stratum of all physical processes, and describes its functions These define the nature of the sub-stratum which is material This is a logical as well as an empirical conclusion If you start with the admission of the reality of the physical world, as physical science does, you must regard its sub-stratum to be material, because otherwise you make the logically fallacious assertion that there can be causal connection between categories entirely different qualitatively When the logically necessary hypothesis about the nature of the sub-stratum of the physical world is empirically established, philosophy has no choice regarding the nature of ultimate reality. The ontological reach of physical knowledge is beyond all possible rational doubt. Scientific knowledge is objective The object of all knowledge is material being and becoming Reality is material. This philosophical consequence of modern physical research can be disputed only through the negation of the very basis of science, namely, the admission of the reality of the physical world

The physical world exists It is not to be constructed by man It is there to be studied, explained, known, understood That is the function of science. Science has performed that function, and has not discovered the roots of physical reality vanishing into nothingness. Its has not reduced matter to mind. It does not reveal matter to be a creation of mind It has proved the self-sufficiency of matter Matter is an objective category. Self-sufficient objectivity is the only reality. Therefore, matter is the only reality It is ontologically real. Its epistemological reality logically follows.